"Neufeld-Erdman writes, 'If God can get along as three Persons, yet one Being, fully differentiated yet united, then we can too!' This hope for the community of faith, expressed through his enthusiasm for the doctrine of the Trinity clearly lies at the heart of *A Table for All*. Indeed, it lies at the heart of Neufeld-Erdman himself. God's unity has become a reality for him as he and members of his congregation have studied and discussed how the gospel relates to LGBT individuals and as he has been challenged to contemplate the Word and words with new eyes. This book is particularly helpful for groups—and many a pastor or group leader will be grateful for the probing discussion questions offered for each chapter."

—MARY LYNN TOBIN
Presbyterian Minister, Leadership Consultant and Coach

"The debate on homosexuality divides the church—a division Jesus prayed against in his high priestly prayer (John 17.20–24). Could it be that the real problem is the division rather than the issue at hand? It's for this reason that the church needs a book like this to help us engage in peaceful dialogue. Neufeld-Erdman has given us a thoughtful and personal reflection that I pray will aid us in becoming the church that Jesus had hoped and prayed for."

—DANNY CORTEZ
pastor, New Heart Community Church (Baptist), La Mirada, CA

"*A Table for All* spills over with the very essence of Jesus's teaching, as Chris Neufeld-Erdman reminds us that to love God and neighbor is the commandment above all others! This heartfelt and slim book calls us back to the basics of our faith; to embrace the essence of the gospel."

—From the Preface by COLLEEN TOWNSEND EVANS
actress (retired) and author

"*A Table for All* delivers an objective and scriptural focus on how gays and lesbians fit into the plan of God. Neufeld-Erdman's work ties together history and Scripture for a comprehensive view of Christ's mission. The result is a read—or really a debate—that engages us to think and re-think a topic we might have thought we'd mastered."

—TIMOTHY PESTOTNIK
Partner, Pestotnik + Gold LLP, Attorneys at Law, San Diego, CA

"The more books we have that testify to the full inclusion of GLBT persons in the church, the better. And the better books we have, the better. If they're written by thoughtful, reflective pastors, all the better. Chris Neufeld-Erdman has joined the rising chorus of church leaders calling for marriage equality and full inclusion. This is a highly readable, small group friendly book, and I heartily recommend it."

—TONY JONES
Theologian and the author of *Did God Kill Jesus?*

"Neufeld-Erdman invites those who embrace biblical authority to journey with him as he comes to a new understanding of God's hospitality. Along the way, he extends a special welcome to those who disagree with his conclusions about God's inclusion of same-gender couples within the marriage covenant. This makes the book a helpful conversation starter for all those wrestling with this very important matter."

—LYNN JOST
Mennonite Brethren pastor and parent of a gay son

"A helpful and easy read for congregational members and church leaders struggling to find a way forward. The book is highly accessible, while providing a biblical, historical, pastoral, and theological path for engaging this issue. Even better, it comes from the extraordinary depth of the author's own wisdom and experience of discerning the nature of the gospel from within a vibrant congregation. It's a testimony that's overdue. Would that many congregations had had it a few years ago! But it will likely help save many from the fracturing that's plaguing the church today and marring its witness."

—JUSTIN SPURLOCK
executive pastor, Columbine United Church, Littleton, CO

A TABLE FOR ALL

A Table for All

How I Came to Understand that
the Gospel Means Full Inclusion
of Gays and Lesbians

Chris Neufeld-Erdman

Foreword by Dr. Gary Demarest
Preface by Colleen Townsend Evans

 CASCADE *Books* · Eugene, Oregon

A TABLE FOR ALL
How I Came to Understand that the Gospel Means Full Inclusion of Gays
and Lesbians

Cascade Books
An Imprint of Wipf and Stock Publishers
199 W. 8th Ave., Suite 3
Eugene, OR 97401

www.wipfandstock.com

ISBN 13: 978-1-4982-0285-5

Cataloguing-in-Publication Data

Neufeld-Erdman, Chris.

A table for all : how I came to understand that the gospel means full inclusion of gays and lesbians / Chris Neufeld-Erdman.

xx + 98 p. ; 23 cm. Includes bibliographical references.

ISBN 13: 978-1-4982-0285-5

1. Homosexuality—Religious aspects—Christianity. 2. Marriage—Biblical
teaching. 3. Christian ethics. I. Title.

BR115.H6 N48 2015

Manufactured in the U.S.A.   02/13/2015

For my son-in-law,

Chris Merrill,

who once said, "I don't understand; how do you get *there*?"

I'm glad you asked.

Chris, I think I finally have a decent answer.

Summary of Contents

FOREWORD BY DR. GARY DEMAREST | xi
PREFACE BY COLLEEN TOWNSEND EVANS | xvii

1. A Testimony and Justification | 1

A tale of two weddings . . . The main questions . . . On keeping faith with the Christian faith . . . On how I was called as an evangelist . . . What evangelists do . . . How the church has often resisted change . . . Is the gospel again breaking down walls? . . . From the heart of an evangelist . . . Why you should read this, even if you disagree.

2. The Bible Says It, Does That Settle It? | 14

On taking the Bible seriously . . . How our congregation engaged the main texts . . . A look at the way Jesus handled the Hebrew Scriptures . . . What we saw as we looked at Leviticus, for example . . . The call to responsible theological work . . . Our interpretive habits need to be evangelized . . . Why "Scripture alone" is not enough.

3. Why We Need History and Reason | 26

Why we need to take history seriously . . . How thoughtful
Christians have changed their minds about many things over
time . . . The early Christological debates . . . Copernicus,
Galileo, the solar system, and church censure . . . The slave
trade, the Bible, and the challenge of the gospel . . . The role
of women in the church . . . On the nature of the Bible and
what we mean by biblical authority . . . Will we take this same
path regarding homosexuality?

4. The Pastoral and Missional Situation | 41

On Saint Paul's and Saint Peter's changes of mind . . . The
slave trade and how William Wilberforce changed his mind
. . . What pastoral experience has shown me . . . The trauma,
fear, and isolation Christian families face . . . On what a truly
evangelical theology requires . . . What we must learn from
the history of Christian mission . . . Why we must take care
that we are not found to be "opposing God" (Acts 5:38).

5. The Trajectory of the Greatest Commandment and the New Creation | 56

We must remain fastened fully to Jesus Christ . . . On the relationship of law and gospel, Old and New . . . Jesus Christ is
creation happening all over again . . . Why Jesus posed such
a problem to the religious of his day . . . How love of God
and love of neighbor sum up Jesus' teaching . . . Saint Paul's
vision of reconciliation and the wideness of God's mercy . . .
On signs of the end of all things.

6. Now What? | 73

How difference of opinion is not a danger to community but a guarantee of its health . . . Marriage is sacred, a sign of the of the way of union . . . How I will uphold the sanctity of marriage . . . On the robust conversations about marriage and sexuality we need today . . . Why a better understanding of the Trinity is essential for the way forward . . . On how we need to reexamine the nature and role of ordination for the twenty-first century.

A Guide for Reflection and Conversation | 78

A guide for personal or group use.

Bibliography | 97

Foreword by Dr. Gary Demarest

I've long hoped for a book just like this. It faces squarely and faithfully a subject so controversial that it's dividing earnest Christians from one another.

I'm now in my late eighties and have served as a pastor for over sixty years. The book makes me recall one of my most treasured memories from my long journey as a pastoral and denominational leader. Almost a decade ago I served as cochair of my denomination's Theological Task Force on the Peace, Unity, and Purity of the Church—a task force entrusted with helping the church through this most challenging of seasons.

The 217th General Assembly of the Presbyterian Church (USA) met in 2006, and by a strong vote adopted our Task Force's final report, receiving it as a guide for congregations and governing bodies to work together discerning and clarifying the nature of our Christian identity and vocation in and for the twenty-first century. Our purpose was to focus on "issues of Christology, biblical authority and interpretation, ordination standards, and power." But we became much more than a mere task force.

Twenty of us from across the Presbyterian Church (USA) met twice a year for three to four days at a time, over a five-year period. We were chosen because each of us was known to have significant theological differences and disagreements from others in the group. Instead of either focusing on our differences or trying to come to consensus, we found something else at work among us. We became a community despite our differences and disagreements. We experienced pain and joy, comfort and discomfort, and, most significantly to me, we discovered that our unity in Jesus Christ did not require agreement on any or all of the issues that confront the church in our time.

We studied Scripture with passion and energy, we prayed and worshiped with love and devotion. In the end, we found that we were unanimous in our sense of gratitude to God for the spiritual growth that each of us experienced through the entire process.

I am deeply grateful for that experience. But I do have one regret. I regret that this immensely transforming experience came to me at the end of my ministry, rather than at its beginning. I will always wish that my entire ministry had been shaped by that journey through difference and disagreement and into a remarkable experience of spiritual unity and friendship with many who I otherwise could have viewed with suspicion and distrust.

You hold in your hands another witness to a similar journey. What's more, it's an invitation to join in. The journey Dr. Chris Neufeld-Erdman describes in this book rings with truth. It narrates the power of the Holy Spirit to create "the peace, unity, and purity" of the body of Christ even when we continue to have conflict and differences among us.

It is my fervent hope that you will not only read this book, but that you will also adopt its model in your own congregation or small group. For pastors, Dr. Neufeld-Erdman models a style of pastoral leadership worthy of emulation. And for us all, pastors and parishioners alike, Neufeld-Erdman models the kind of courage we need in order to face our fears whenever we are invited by God to consider the possibility that we might need to change our minds.

Chris is clearly centered in Jesus Christ without being dogmatic. He's clearly committed to the authority of the Scriptures without being authoritarian in his interpretation and application of them.

He's both prophetic and pastoral. He articulates his convictions clearly and, at the same time, shows respect and love for any and all who are unable to arrive at his conclusions, which are the fruit of his long and courageous journey. His pastoral skill is something I know personally, having experienced it firsthand when he led my extended family through a time of deep and painful crisis.

The fact is, the inclusion of gays and lesbians as full participants in the church, or their exclusion from it, can no longer be ignored or postponed—particularly in the growing number of states in which marriage is recognized as a civil right for all people.

The church can no longer dance around this issue.

Each pastor and each congregation must say "yes" or "no." Saying, "You're gay and you're welcome here, but you can't live a normal life—you can't marry or be fully involved in the life of the church unless you become, or at least act, straight" will simply not do. Not in today's world, and not if we, as Chris so clearly argues, are going to live in faithfulness to the gospel of Jesus Christ.

Chris Neufeld-Erdman has offered his unequivocal "yes" and put it right out in front—in the subtitle of this book. And I'm deeply grateful!

But what I admire most is his willingness and courage to change his mind.

Look, I'm considered old now. I'm late into my ninth decade. And I'm chastened by the fact that I still seem to have an insatiable need to be right, and I'm haunted by a crippling fear of being wrong. For most of my life I've been driven by an inner need to establish my rightness and to deny any hint of wrongness.

As I look back over my life, I'm humbled that one of the first speeches I ever made in a denominational setting was the time I, as a young pastor, stood up at a presbytery meeting (our local gathering of pastors and elders of area churches) to oppose, on biblical grounds, the ordination of women clergy.

I summoned my best biblical exegesis to advance my argument. I made a strong case for the historic and orthodox position. And then, when the vote was taken, and much to my chagrin, I lost. The majority wasn't impressed by my rhetoric or my impassioned appeal to the rightness of my argument.

I've long since changed my mind about women in ministry, though I can't remember the particular moment or occasion when that change occurred. I take the Bible just as seriously now as I did then, though I interpret and apply it differently. And though I've celebrated with joy, respect, gratitude, and collegiality the full inclusion of women as clergy for many years, I realize that some congregations and denominations, both in the United States and globally, still do not ordain women as clergy or leaders. I disagree with them, but I respect their right to hold their convictions.

Over the course of my long ministry, I've also changed my mind about divorce. Early on, I refused to perform marriages for divorced people on the basis of my interpretation of what were, to me, clear biblical teachings. Then divorce came knocking at my door. I'm grateful to those who loved me and helped me through that process and finally into a healing marriage that's thriving after more than fifty-five years. My interpretation and application of those same Scriptures I once used to exclude divorced people has changed because, like Peter, who heard the knocking of the Holy Spirit on the door of his life (Acts 10), I too had a personal experience that sent me back to the Bible to learn what God might say to those who find themselves broken and isolated by the pain of marital failure.

Recently, I revisited portions of two commentaries I wrote on Colossians (*Colossians: The Mystery of Christ in Us*, 1979) and Leviticus (*Leviticus,* The Preacher's Commentary, 2004). I'm not at all reluctant to say that my understanding of human sexuality, particularly relating to gays and lesbians, has changed substantially since then. And I'm grateful that I'm able to walk in the company of those who, like the Apostles Peter and Paul and so many like them, are able to change their minds—Christians who are driven neither by an insatiable need to be forever right, nor by the crippling fear of the possibility of being wrong.

I'm grateful that Chris Neufeld-Erdman stands tall in that company.

One of my heroes in that company was John MacKay (1889–1983)—the great Scottish Presbyterian leader, former missionary to South America, and president of Princeton Theological Seminary. He became a mentor and treasured friend to me in his later years.

I'll never forget the last conversation we shared just before his death. It was a cold day in Georgetown and MacKay walked me to my car, bundled up in topcoat and earmuffs. As I prepared to drive off, he leaned into me and said: "Remember, Gary, hold fast to Jesus Christ, and stay loose with all the rest."

I'm now eighty-eight years old. And though I've still got plenty of energy for ministry and am still serving as an interim pastor during this tumultuous season of the church's life, I feel a bit like John Mackay. I'm nearing the end of a great life, and I see Christ more fully than ever before.

And so I say to you: Pick up this little book. It's a rare gem for the churches at this point in time. Read it well and read it with others. Debate it. Challenge it. Delight in it. But don't dismiss either its message or those who see things differently than you do. Give yourself and others freedom to agree or disagree.

Remember, friend, in everything "hold fast to Jesus Christ, and stay loose with all the rest."

Preface by Colleen Townsend Evans

Author of numerous books on the Christian life including *A Deeper Joy*.

There is more to this personal, heartfelt, slim volume than the exploration of an issue that has become contentious in the life of our church today.

A Table for All spills over with the very essence of Jesus' teaching, as Chris Neufeld-Erdman shines light on the commandment above all others—to love God and neighbor. And "neighbor" as defined by Jesus in his parable of the Good Samaritan is one who is different from ourselves.

As a teenager, I made a commitment to Jesus Christ. It was the most important decision of my life, and the challenge and joy of that decision continues to this day. But, make no mistake, sometimes following Jesus can be very scary.

I became a member of the Presbyterian Church in 1948 (quite awhile ago). Many seasons have passed. There have been many challenges. Throughout all these years I have been grateful, along with my lifelong love and pastor husband, to be part of a Big Tent church. A church firmly anchored in Jesus Christ, while welcoming people very different from one another. People who look, act, think, and often feel very differently about issues of the day. My conviction, then and now, is that it is not "sameness" that unites us. It is our common love of God, in Jesus Christ. I also believe that a congregation that not only allows diversity but celebrates it is a richer community, as it reflects the way Jesus loves and accepts people across every conceivable line. The Spirit makes us one! (Ephesians 2:13)

Conversely, I know that for myself, if I allow conflict over diverse views to sever relationships, it is most likely a sign that I have shifted my focus from Christ and his greatest command to lesser issues.

A Table for All calls us back to the basics of our faith. Chris challenges us to come together around the table, even with our differences, and love our way through this season of conflict. If we can do this, the world might take notice, and more important, God will be honored by obedience to his command. To love wholeheartedly—both God and neighbor.

"Then Peter began to speak to them: 'I truly understand
that God shows no partiality,
but in every nation anyone who fears God and does what is right is
acceptable to God.'"

ACTS 10:34–35

"Now in Christ Jesus you who once were far off
have been brought near by the blood of Christ."

EPHESIANS 2:13

1

A Testimony and Justification

1. The young man looked into the mirror, smiled nervously, and straightened his tie. It was his wedding day, and for just these few moments, he was alone in the washroom. He breathed deeply and looked himself over. "Well, buddy," he said out loud, "this is it; this is for real." As a teenager, he'd babysat my children, been active in our youth group, and worked for several summers at our Presbyterian camp in the California mountains—at one point, living there year-round as part of the camp staff. Over the years, both his parents served on the governing board of our church, leading a number of different ministries. He and his family were as active in the life of the church as any family could be. But when he "came out," all that changed. Feeling judged and unwelcome among Presbyterians, he'd have left the faith entirely, if not for the Episcopalians. So, when California state law opened the door to marriage equality, he and his fiancé married each other at the local Episcopal church, whose clergy were permitted to marry gay Christians, and where they had been warmly welcomed and gathered in. Even if we Presbyterians

hadn't alienated him, we still, as of early June 2014, had a policy against same-gender marriage. And so, the two young lovers couldn't get married among the congregation that helped raise him, the people among whom he and his parents and his sister had worshiped and served Jesus Christ.

2. His parents bravely made his wedding public, inviting relatives, friends, and church folk—and no small amount of whispered "concern" about the moral and doctrinal appropriateness of all this ensued. Regardless, a good number of those invited showed up for the celebration, despite their reservations and discomfort. But there were some who refused, on *principle,* to attend. For those who did attend, it was a remarkable experience. One of our elders told me afterward that he was deeply moved by the ceremony: "The most traditional wedding I've ever attended. Right out of the Anglican *Book of Common Prayer,*" he said. "A liturgy four hundred years old."

3. The next weekend, another couple associated with our church got married. A man and a woman. A contemporary service. Outside, at a ranch. The only excuse for not attending this wedding was the problem of prior commitments. No one questioned it on principle—that is, morally or doctrinally. No one wondered if this wedding was right and good and faithful. There were no questions asked, period.

4. But for an increasing number of Americans this is changing. Many people I know are asking questions like: Is one of these marriages wrong in the eyes of God and the other right? Do people today really have to hold the line on traditional marriage against dramatic cultural shifts? Does God really want us to continue excluding gays and lesbians from

so great a gift as marriage? Could we see things today that our ancestors couldn't see? Has the time come for us to change our convictions about same-gender marriage much the same way scientists in the sixteenth century changed their views, despite warnings by church officials, about the planets and stars and earth's relationship to them? And many Christians wonder if the old prohibition against gays and lesbians serving as elders and deacons and pastors still makes sense given the fruitful lives of gay and lesbian friends and family members and coworkers.

5. With new questions in mind and without solid answers, many of those who were once connected to Christianity are dropping out, and those who might otherwise be drawn to Christ are repelled by Christianity. The kind of judgmentalism, hypocrisy, and narrow-mindedness they experience among religious people is a turnoff. On the other hand, there are committed Christians who are motivated by other questions. Deeply alarmed by this cultural shift, they want to know how to stop it and how to save the faith from the moral relativism they see all around them. Some of them are organizing in strong opposition to trends they perceive as morally abhorrent, theologically unsound, and spiritually dangerous. Others, while concerned, are not hostile or vocal in their opposition. Instead, they quietly worry that the church is losing its way. Many of them are praying for a conservative recovery; they want churches where the lines are more clearly drawn, and they're hoping they can stay put in the congregations they have loved and served. But, frustratingly for them, they don't see and hear much that gives them any real hope their pastors will guard their flocks from these corrupting moral forces and lead them back to more historic convictions.

6. So we are at a watershed moment. We need solid answers that aren't mere echoes of the wrangling of the Far Right or Left—the defensive kind of posturing that shadows the polarization current in our nation's politics. We need thoughtful, grounded reflection born from the struggle of trying to discern the truth in the midst of real dialogue with people across the spectrum, those who hold opposing opinions and differing experiences but who are seeking to live in faithfulness to the ways of God revealed in Jesus Christ.

7. What follows is my attempt to answer this need. It's essentially a testimony to my growth in understanding both the human drama and the divine desire for wholeness and holiness with respect to homosexuality and the gospel. It's a witness to my understanding of the nature of homosexuality and the nature of the gospel, the authority of the Bible and its interpretation throughout history, the pastoral needs of LGBT persons and their families, and the missional issues facing the church today. Finally, it's a witness to my understanding of the theological core of Christianity found in the teachings of Jesus and Saint Paul. It is this core, this rule of faith, that makes it possible for Christians today to keep faith with our historic faith and find in it a vision for the full inclusion of those the church has too long marginalized and excluded. I have come to understand, as Saint Peter so memorably put it, "that God shows no partiality, but in every nation anyone who fear him and does what is right is acceptable to him" (Acts 10:34–35). This is not only true for the Gentiles, who were once excluded from the grace and covenants of God, but also for those whose sexual orientation has for too long distanced them from the wholeness and holiness they seek and need. Gays and lesbians, no less than

anyone else, were once far off, but now "have been brought near by the blood of Christ" (Eph 2:13).

8. For a number of Christians, that statement isn't just off-putting, it's a deal breaker. In fact, if it offends you, you may well stop reading right here. "Why continue reading something," you might ask, "if I already know it to be wrong?" Because this issue isn't going away. Neither is your duty as a Christian to have an answer rooted in your understanding of the gospel. So if you disagree with my position and continue to do so after reading this book, you at least will better understand what you believe and why. What's more, you will better understand those who hold a different viewpoint from your own, and maybe you will be able to honor them as sisters and brothers in Christ even though you may not like their theology. Saint Paul said, "If it is possible, so far as it depends on you, live peaceably with all" (Rom 12:18), and "in humility regard others as better than yourselves" (Phil 2:3). We Christians must do our best to understand each other, even though we do not always agree with each other.

9. What follows is essentially a story. It won't always be a narrative; I'll work on texts and explore history and talk theology, but always in the framework of my own story of change, the opening of my eyes to behold the beauty and power of the gospel, the generosity and compassion of Jesus Christ. It's not unlike the conversion of Saint Paul or the transformation of Saint Peter. And, as with them, the change happened in and through community—face-to-face with real people struggling to be both human and Christian.

10. The people of my former congregation, University Presbyterian Church, were important in this change and growth.

We spent the bulk of 2010 in a congregational study called "The Bible and Homosexuality"—a course attended widely, not only by our own people, but also by interested people from the larger community. Designed by a judge, psychotherapist, church historian, and theologian, it was a strong and balanced study, intended to avoid polarizing people. We wanted to lay out the issues and explore them fully, but not to promote one view over the other. I think it was profoundly important to us and that it did immense good, even though some people left the church because they couldn't be a part of conversations about what was clearly wrong to them.

11. This disciplined study with that congregation, combined with deeply personal and pastoral encounters with gay and lesbian persons and their families, has brought me to this place of testimony. I offer it up for those who have questions that simply won't go away, and who are looking for ways to be deeply Christian *and* broadly welcoming and inclusive. I also offer it to people in congregations who hold traditional and conservative views, but who are genuinely interested in how people like me, firmly committed to Jesus Christ and the Bible, can possibly believe such things. That said, I'll return to the story . . .

12. For nearly twenty-five years, I've been a pastor—guiding, growing, and praying two different congregations into the fullness of Christ's gospel during a long season of significant global change. I've now begun my ministry in the third and possibly last congregation I'll serve. I love being a pastor, and wouldn't swap it for anything, but my call to ministry was initially a call to be an evangelist, and I've never lost that passion.

13. I was a young man when I was called as an evangelist. A recent business school graduate, I was in charge of marketing operations for a small start-up software company in Denver. I was also a member of the Corona Presbyterian Church. I'd come to faith in Jesus Christ seven years earlier, at the end of my senior year of high school. Up until then I'd been an atheist, staunchly so. I was certain there was no God and that religious people were gullible, foolish, and backward. But atheism gave me no comfort. Humanity was a blip on the screen of cosmic history, an accident of nature. The universe was a zillion years old and filled with billions of stars and planets. In the midst of it all, I was essentially nothing. That reality, added to my teenage angst, left me feeling terribly alone. All that changed suddenly when God broke through and opened me up to the reality of Jesus Christ. Jesus changed my life, and I knew then that in Christ, the light that created the cosmos is available to every lost and lonely person who doesn't know how immensely valuable and loved he or she is. Jesus Christ makes us whole and is making all things whole.

14. One Saturday morning in the mid-1980s, I was to join a couple of other young men from my church while I preached the gospel on street corners at Denver's famed People's Fair. I was nervous as I searched the crowds for my friends. I never found them, and I didn't preach the gospel that day. But I did stand at the top of the stairs of Denver's East High School, looking out over the crowd. I wept. I felt overwhelmed, even afraid, yet full of awe as Christ showed me a vision of this teeming mass of humanity one in Christ, reconciled to God. Christ planted within me a seed of longing—what almost felt like a wound (and still does)—for every human being to know Christ and experience the new creation begun in him. That night, I read in my Bible the words, "As the Father sent

me, so I am sending you" (John 20:21). It was the moment I knew myself to be called by God as an evangelist.

15. I was young then and dreamed of preaching to stadiums full of people—people streaming down from their seats, tears in their eyes, drawn to Christ. It was the only kind of evangelism I knew—that and handing out tracts. I needed to do more than hand out tracts, so in obedience to the vision and the word of God, I left my work as a businessman and trained for pastoral ministry. For a quarter century now, I've worked as a pastor, but I've never ceased to be an evangelist. My heart is still for those who don't know Christ, don't understand the gospel, and who find themselves alienated from the church. I long to see the teeming mass of the left out, thrown out, burned out, and down-and-out made whole in Jesus Christ.

16. Scripture and history testify that evangelists can find themselves running into trouble. Evangelists are often prophets who cut a new path, chart a new way, open doors previously closed by prejudice and intolerance. Jesus was such an evangelist and his preaching of the reign of God put him on a collision course with the religious authorities of his day. The Apostle Paul, who, after zealously persecuting the church, completely changed his mind, and was persecuted for his vision of the new humanity in Christ where the walls of separation between people groups were erased by the reconciling power of Jesus Christ. Like Paul before him, the Bishop William Seymour preached Christ in the early 1900s to mixed audiences of men and women, blacks and whites and other races during the Azusa Street revival in Los Angeles. He was sternly denounced by those in authority over him. His work was called the work of the devil because of

his tolerance of race and gender mixing in his evangelistic services.

17. Evangelists don't just preach a heavenly message of hope in the hereafter while allowing injustice to keep people in chains, prejudice to go unchallenged, and the principalities and powers to keep divided what Christ has united. Evangelists are heralds of the reign of God, and catalysts of new communities springing up in Christ as witnesses to the seed of wholeness and reconciliation planted in the world through the person and work of Jesus Christ. Evangelists bring change, and there have always been opponents who don't like the fact that they "who have turned the world upside down have come here too" (Acts 17:6).

18. Over the course of history the church has been confronted with the realities of race and ethnicity, power and wealth, war and violence, science and philosophy, intellectual currents of the day, cultural trends and shifts. In these encounters the church has too often been afraid of the world, resistant to change. It's too often viewed itself as something separate from a world destined for hell. At its worst moments, it's judged the world. Drawn lines. Created walls. It's been quick to point out sin, while ignoring real evil. It's done this despite its constitution in a gospel that moves in the other direction—always toward mercy, not judgement; compassion, not condemnation; reconciliation, wholeness, and unity, not division. (I'll explore this trajectory of the gospel more fully later.) In its encounter with the world, the church has often been forced, sometimes against its will by the lonely voices of evangelists and prophets, to work out the implications of the gospel in its particular time and place. Like Saints Paul and Peter early on, the church has had to

change its mind. And there are few in the church today who do not acknowledge, in hindsight, that those changes were prompted by the Holy Spirit. We need only to mention the astronomer Galileo (1564–1642) to remember that beliefs that once seemed wrong, offensive, and even heretical as late as the seventeenth century have become normative.[1] And practices like the human slave trade, so common in the eighteenth and nineteenth centuries, and justified biblically, are now viewed universally as crimes against humanity and an assault against the image of God in every human person (again, I'll explore this more fully in a later section).

19. I believe our current struggle in society and in the church over gay rights, marriage, and ordination will follow the same path. We will come to recognize not only the God-given dignity of homosexual persons, but also the goodness and holiness of faithful, monogamous marriages between persons of nondominant sexual orientations. More and more Americans now support marriage equality, and an increasing number of state governments recognize same-gender marriage. And while a majority of Christians around the world still do not, an increasing number of Christian leaders, like Pope Francis, for example, no longer speak against homosexuality in the harsh tones of the past. Some, like Archbishop Desmond Tutu, are stepping forward to declare that the church's

---

1. Galileo Galilei was a sixteenth- and seventeenth-century Italian mathematician, astronomer, and scientist who ran afoul of the church because he taught what was then thought to be clearly contrary to Scripture. Scripture, the church declared, taught that the earth is the center of the solar system and the sun and planets revolve around it. Galileo, on the other hand, disagreed. His scientific observations made it clear that the sun was the center of the solar system, while the earth was merely one of the planets in revolution around the sun. In 1615, the Roman Inquisition denounced Galileo's discoveries as false and contrary to Scripture, forcing Galileo to recant and identifying him as a heretic.

past position is untenable and contrary to the gospel. A number of denominations are stepping forward too. In June 2014, my own Presbyterian denomination approved a policy that allows clergy to perform marriages for gay couples in states that allow it.

20. Inspired by the gospel and informed by history, it is time for me as an evangelist and pastor to step forward too, and testify to what I see and hear in the gospel of our Lord Jesus Christ. The gospel is breaking down new walls of exclusion and intolerance in our day, despite the anger and even violent resistance to these changes by religious believers. Homosexual persons, no less than heterosexual persons, are full and acceptable inheritors of the abundance of God offered in Jesus Christ.

21. Though things are changing, I realize that many Christians will be deeply troubled by my testimony. But it's not the first time such a thing has happened, and it won't be the last. I realize that I will be misunderstood, maligned, and likely attacked as a Christian leader who has lost the way, veered from the path, and departed from tradition. Colleagues and church members will dismiss what I have to say. (I understand—for a long time I avoided serious reflection on these matters because I thought I knew what the Bible clearly taught.) But I ask those who will dismiss me: did Isaiah lose his way when he declared, against the Mosaic law, that in the "new thing" God is doing, even eunuchs (the sexually estranged) are welcome in the house of God? (Isa 56:3–5) Or, did Isaiah see the tradition anew and in the light of the vision of the new creation given to him by the Lord? Did Jesus lose his way when he broke the commandments in order to show the love and mercy and justice of God? Did Saint Paul

lose his way when he preached the gospel to the Gentiles at a time when the early Jewish Christians still assumed Jesus was for Jews? Did Luther lose his way?[2] Did Wilberforce?[3] Did Aimee Semple McPherson?[4] Did Dr. King?[5] Did Desmond Tutu?[6] There have been many who were quite sure that each of these lost their way, departed from tradition, and were dangerous disturbers of the church, leading many astray. And they made these reformers suffer for it. But none of these reformers yielded their holy vision to the forces of intimidation. They were each drawn into the larger force of God's continual reformation of the church, a force they could not resist while still remaining faithful to Jesus Christ.

22. Today, there's a largely unreached tribe whom Christ loves and wants to gather in. It's a tribe that's at best ignored, at worst abhorred. I not only aim to reach them for Christ's sake but to ensure they belong in all their dignity and beauty, enriching the body of Christ with their gifts, and in doing so advance God's reign by cultivating a community where anyone drawn to Christ receives an unmistakable, unqualified invitation to come and eat at the table of the Lord among an ever-growing circle of friends.

2. In 1516, Martin Luther, a Catholic monk and theology professor, posted his Ninety-Five Theses on the castle door at Wittenberg and catalyzed the Protestant Reformation's break from Roman Catholicism.

3. William Wilberforce was a leader in the British abolitionist movement; he fought against slavery despite the "clear" teaching of Scripture on the matter.

4. Aimee Semple McPherson was an early-twentieth-century American evangelist and pastor—an early advocate of the full equality and authority of women in ministry.

5. The Rev. Dr. Martin Luther King Jr. was a leader of the 1960s civil rights movement that was violently opposed by white southern Christians.

6. The Archbishop of Cape Town, South Africa, who along with Nelson Mandela led the protest against apartheid, a chief doctrine of the Dutch Reformed Church in South Africa.

23. If you're serious about the gospel and desire to see the reign of God extend to more and more of creation; if you're concerned about the next generations and their receptivity to the gospel; if you're willing to admit that God has moved the church to overturn and evangelize old ideas and habits in ways that disturbed Christians at the time, I hope you'll read on. Test my ideas. Wrestle honestly with them. I haven't come to this place without considerable wrestling and struggle. You may find yourself agreeing with them. Then again, you may not. But you will have thought and prayed about the implications of the gospel today, and will be better able to articulate your position in a society and church where issues of gay marriage and the ordination of gay and lesbian persons are not going to go away.

2

The Bible Says It,
Does That Settle It?

24. All Christians take Scripture seriously, but we Protestant Christians have a history of taking it particularly seriously. The Protestant Reformation was reformation based essentially on Scripture above all else. The Reformation championed a return to the singular authority of the Bible against the intrusion of lesser authorities like tradition and human opinion, experience, and even reason and common sense, which all seemed to the Reformers to make the church vulnerable to subjectivity and open to deception. Over the course of my ministry and in the congregations I've served, the great watchword of the Reformation, "Scripture alone," has held pride of place. It's kept my congregations and me connected to the larger story of our theological heritage.

25. And so, when we found ourselves unavoidably faced with the issue of homosexuality in the wider culture and in the church, we, like good Swiss Calvinists and children of the Reformation, turned to the Bible. Our nearly year-long

congregational study, "The Bible and Homosexuality," was our answer. As I said earlier, a number of our people were appalled. How could we spent nine months, they wondered, on a topic that ought to be settled in a matter of minutes—by reading a handful of Bible passages that put that matter in no uncertain terms? But others, like our Scottish Presbyterian ancestors who ardently resisted both king and pope, realized they didn't want to to be told what to think by others; they wanted to determine the truth for themselves. And they wanted to determine the truth by turning to the Bible. So we picked it up, but not by simply opening its pages. First, we did the important and often neglected work of learning the art, or science, of biblical interpretation in the Reformed tradition. People realized that they had never really learned how to interpret the Bible. They knew how to read it. They had let others interpret it for them. But they hadn't really considered that reading Scripture can't be done rightly by simply opening it up and reading it. People have done crazy things by reading the Bible without wisdom. We explored a number of these things in order to help each other approach the biblical texts associated with homosexuality with as few biases as possible; we wanted to let the Bible speak for itself, and learn to set aside our opinions, prejudices, and agendas.

26. Then, after laying the groundwork for responsible biblical interpretation in the Reformed tradition, we entered into an extended season of engagement with the biblical texts themselves. Our goal was to engage them slowly, ensuring that we were not merely seeing what we had always seen. But neither were we looking for innovative, unconventional interpretations. We just were not in a hurry and allowed ourselves to linger in these biblical texts.

27. We studied Genesis 1–2, Genesis 19, Leviticus 18–20, Romans 1, 1 Corinthians 6, 1 Timothy 1, and Isaiah 56/Matthew 19 (regarding eunuchs). These sessions were led by our own pastors, as well as university and seminary faculty. All these texts, except Genesis 19, address homosexuality explicitly. (Most scholars agree that Genesis 19 addresses the sin of inhospitality, which in the Middle East is a serious matter. Genesis 19 addresses homosexuality indirectly, that is, it is not the main issue in the text.) Overall, reading these texts, we found that the verdict of the Bible regarding homosexuality seems clear—*it's not for it.*

28. That said, what also became clear to most of us is that what the Bible denounced as sinful homosexual acts *may* be different from the kind of homosexuality we encounter among our gay and lesbian family members, friends, neighbors, students, and coworkers. That word, *may*, is very important, because, among people concerned to interpret the Bible faithfully as the Word of God, the word *may* raises an important yellow flag. It says: slow down, caution, not so fast. We who presume to speak for God in today's world don't want to speak wrongly in God's name—too much of that's been done in the past. For, if we hold up a doctrine as God's word, and that doctrine is more closely tied to our own opinions, assumptions, and cultural practices than it is to God's revelation in Jesus Christ, then we are not "faithfully handling the Word of God" (2 Tim 2:15) and there are serious consequences for that failure.[1]

---

1. See 1 Timothy 1:3–9 for Saint Paul's instruction to Timothy about the way many who presume to be faithful interpreters of God's Word are not. Note also how this warning comes just prior to one of the classic texts presuming to prohibit homosexuality.

29. We began our biblical study in Genesis. Many people look to the first two chapters of Genesis when setting out the agenda for marriage and human sexuality. Genesis 1:27 declares that "God created humankind in his image, in the image of God he created them; male and female he created them," and in Genesis 2:18–25 we read of the incompleteness Adam experienced until, from Adam's own body, God created Eve. "Therefore," Genesis says, "a man leaves his father and his mother and clings to his wife, and they become one flesh" (2:24). Apparently, the complementarity of male and female is woven into the structure of creation. "But," asked one person during our study of this text, "does that mean that those who experience the delight Adam found in Eve,[2] but find it in a person of the same gender, are experiencing something contrary to God's design? Or could it be that same-gender marital relationships were simply not on the radar at that point in history? You realize, don't you," the participant continued, "that there's no reference in the New Testament to a woman receiving the Lord's Supper. It's always men. I suppose you could argue that because no woman explicitly receives holy communion in the Bible that we ought to send the women out of the room during the communion part of our services. But who in the world would recommend *that*? I think we ought to take care not to simply assume, based on this text, that marriage is only for a man and a woman." Another participant added, "And I think, based on Genesis, that we also ought to take care not to hold up 'marriage according to Genesis.' After all, there's Abraham, who had *several* wives; Jacob too. Do we really want to say that Genesis—or any other part of the Old Testament—holds the model for

---

2. "Then the man said, 'This at last is bone of my bones and flesh of my flesh!'" (Gen 2:23).

modern Christian marriage? I mean, look at David . . . or Solomon."

30. These were important questions, questions that came from taking the Bible very seriously, and realizing that we often import uncritically into the Bible our own prejudices, habits, and practices.

31. So for help, we turned to Jesus himself, who refers to this text from Genesis in Matthew 19:3–5 when answering the Pharisees' question about divorce. "Have you not read," he asked the religious authorities of his day, "that the one who made them at the beginning 'made them male and female,' and said, 'For this reason a man will leave his father and mother and be joined to his wife, and the two will become one flesh.'"

32. We wondered, was Jesus quoting Genesis because he was validating heterosexuality as the *only* norm for lifelong sexual unions? Or, was he merely recognizing what was normal and common to his audience in order to move on to his more revolutionary teaching about God's reign? Many of us came to see that the context argues for the latter. In the immediate context, he was challenging at least three things. First, he was challenging the "hardheartedness" of the Pharisees and their husband-benefiting practice of no-fault divorce (19:7–9); a man could simply and abruptly divorce a woman, no questions asked, leaving her marginalized and extremely vulnerable. Second, he challenged their attitudes toward eunuchs (males castrated so that, as servants among the rich and powerful, they wouldn't mess around with their master's wives). According to the law of Moses, eunuchs were excluded from the Hebrew religion (Deut 23:1), but in an astonishing theological and

moral turn in the prophecy of Isaiah, they were welcomed in among the faithful (Isa 56:1–8). Third and finally, Jesus challenged the religiously serious of his day about their treatment of children (19:13–15). In fact, the larger sweep of the rest of his teaching in this section undermines traditional Pharisaical practice and challenges their thinking for the sake of a way of life that includes those previously excluded. We saw this clearly in the parable that concludes this section of Matthew: the landowner, who represents God, says, "'Am I not allowed to do what I choose with what belongs to me? Or are you envious because I am generous?' So the last will be first, and the first will be last" (20:15–16).

33. Our close reading of Genesis 1–2, and in particular the way Jesus interacted with it when engaged in a debate about marriage, showed me, at least, that Jesus himself did not appeal to Genesis in order to teach about marriage. He was not teaching that marriage is between Adam and Eve, not Adam and Steve—that is, his reference to Scripture was not to teach heterosexuality as the norm for marriage. Rather, he used the text in order to subvert the Pharisaical understanding and practice of marriage (and other things) and point to the reign of God. Homosexuality wasn't on his radar screen. He wasn't grounding marriage in the structure of creation, he was addressing the abuse of women, the sexually wounded, as well as children. And he was challenging the misuse of Scripture and tradition to justify these abuses.

34. When we came to the laws in Leviticus, we found interpreting these texts, quite frankly, extremely challenging. We realized that most of us walk among these laws the way we walk through a line at a cafeteria—we pick and choose what we like or that's useful to us, and ignore the rest. For example,

Leviticus 20:13 clearly says that "If a man lies with a male as with a woman, both of them have committed an abomination. They are to be put to death." However, there are many laws prohibiting acts and labeling them as an abomination—from eating certain kinds of leftovers, to eating certain kinds of birds (7:18, 11:13, 19:7, 20:25). Christians today have no qualms about violating these prohibitions. And there are plenty of other Mosaic laws we ignore or dismiss—practicing the Sabbath (Deut 5:12–15), cutting our hair (Lev 19:27), touching a pig (Lev 11:6–8), eating shellfish (Lev 11:10),[3] as well as farming and weaving practices (Lev 19:19)[4]—to name only a few. Of course, there's great scholarly debate about the intention of these commands and all kinds of interpretive trickery that those on both the Right and Left use to justify the dismissal of some laws and the necessity of others for believers today. Some have tried to divide the laws into categories—ceremonial, civil, and moral law—and used these categories to determine which to obey today and which to ignore. A close reading of these laws forced many of us to wonder if this kind of exegetical maneuvering isn't kind of like straining at gnats while swallowing camels (Matt 23:24), or trying to point out the speck in your neighbor's eye, while ignoring the log in your own (Matt 7:3–5). The point is, many of us began to wonder if our approach to these laws is simply too arbitrary and self-serving—like eating at a cafeteria. A commandment that is important to one person isn't to another, and so on.

---

3. "But anything in the seas or the streams that does not have fins and scales, of the swarming creatures in the waters and among all the other living creatures that are in the waters—they are detestable to you." Does this mean Christians can't eat lobster or clams?

4. "You shall keep my statutes. You shall not let your animals breed with a different kind; you shall not sow your field with two kinds of seed; nor shall you put on a garment made of two different materials." Does this mean a cotton blend shirt is off-limits, and if I wear one I should be killed?

35. When it came to the New Testament Scriptures (Rom 1:26–27, 1 Cor 6:9–11, and 1 Tim 1:9–11), we found that while these texts condemn homoerotic sexuality, they do not appear to have in mind what we understand homosexuality to be today. In Romans 1, for example, Saint Paul says, "For this reason God gave them up to degrading passions. Their women exchanged natural intercourse for unnatural, and in the same way also the men, giving up natural intercourse with women, were consumed with passion for one another. Men committed shameless acts with men and received in their own persons the due penalty for their error." Saint Paul's teaching seems quite clear. But as with Genesis, our people, reading the text closely and trying to avoid drawing our modern meanings into the ancient world of the Bible, stepped back and asked, "What is Paul really addressing?" We learned that he was likely condemning a practice known as pederasty, which was common in the Roman Empire and was often integrated into religious life. A Roman adult male could, without censure, engage in penetrative sexual acts with a younger male as long as the younger was not a family member, not a freeborn Roman citizen, and as long as the older male maintained a position of power over the younger and did not become the passive partner. This practice was normal and condoned. The Romans seem to have had more flexible gender categories than we do today. For example, there are no words in Latin for our modern words *homosexual* or *heterosexual,* which is why many historians now refer to Greco-Roman same-sex behavior as *homogenital* or *homoerotic,* and not homosexual, which implies orientation.

36. Of course, this doesn't mean that Saint Paul can be thought to affirm homosexuality as we know it, but it does mean that we cannot simply claim, on Paul's authority, that

all homosexual acts are sinful and all homosexuals are sin-
ners deserving God's wrath. It's a fact that Saint Paul does
not address the kind of monogamous, faithful relationships
our gay friends and family members enjoy or would like to
enjoy. What this work in the biblical texts taught me personally is that faithfulness to Holy Scripture and to the gospel
require me as a pastor, theologian, and evangelist to slow the
church down, help us take a deeper look, and do responsible
theological work.

37. This review of the key texts was important to our congregation. It loosened many of us from the answers we once
thought were so assured by the Bible. But what particularly
challenged me was not the texts from the Law of Moses, the
prophets, and Saint Paul, but what I began to see and hear
from the Lord Jesus himself as I preached from the Gospels
over the next few years.

38. The truth is, when it came to the Law of Moses, our Lord
Jesus Christ held those laws loosely. The Gospels present Jesus as the great lawbreaker (Mark 2:23–28). They show him
to be remarkably willing to dismiss scriptural laws when
they were causing injury to others. He defended a woman
caught in adultery and who was, according to Scripture, to
be stoned to death—and he summoned to a higher ethic
those who sought to uphold a text of Scripture that required
her death (John 8:2–11). He healed the sick on the sabbath in
a flagrant disregard for sabbath commands (Mark 3:1–6). He
ate and drank with the despised and sinful (Luke 5:27–32).
He confronted the religiously pious about their commitment
to laws that put heavy burdens on the backs of others while
doing nothing to reach those in misery with the good news
of God's compassion, love, and justice (Matt 23:1–36). Jesus'

opponents fought him because they thought he presumed to be above the law. In fact, Jesus didn't claim to be above it. Instead he claimed to be the fulfillment of the law, the true interpreter of the law (Matt 5:17–18). The writer of the Letter to the Hebrews teaches Jewish Christians that Jesus supercedes Moses, that the gospel replaces the law (Hebrews 3:1–6). This doesn't mean that the law is irrelevant. No, Jesus himself said, "Do not think that I have come to abolish the law or the prophets; I have come not to abolish but to fulfill" (Matt 5:17). What is clear from the New Testament is that Christians, like Jesus, must practice an artful interpretive dance as we read the law in the light of the gospel. And the way we deal with the law will not always make religious people happy. We see this in the ministry of Jesus. His artful dance with the law stirred up violent opposition to his mission and ministry, and led to his death.

39. This look at Jesus made me, along with others, wonder why we work so determinedly to figure out exactly what the commands in the Hebrew Scriptures say about homosexuality, when Jesus seemed not merely ambivalent toward so many of those laws, but often hostile to them. Jesus seems to make things much simpler than we make them today. One law above all others seemed to be the sole key to his understanding of all biblical commands: "You shall love the Lord your God with all your heart and soul and mind and strength, and love your neighbor as yourself" (Luke 10:27).

40. Jesus called this the Greatest Commandment for a reason; it's more than a biblical sound bite. It is embedded alongside one of the most important and memorable stories in the Bible, a story that further clarifies what Jesus means by it. The story begins with a young expert in the law who came

to test Jesus' orthodoxy, but who, by story's end, is himself supremely tested by Jesus. The story ends with the parable of the Good Samaritan. Through that parable, Luke gives the church a clue about how it is to handle Holy Scripture in ways that are truly faithful to the God who authorized it. And, according to the story, Jesus' interpretive approach is not often in accord with the approach of the Bible teachers (the lawyers) of Jesus' day. In the parable, Jesus exposes the religious authorities and guardians of the law (the priest and Levite) as moral failures who, captive to old ways of reading the Bible, are unwilling to live out the ultimate law, the Greatest Commandment.

41. Instead, Jesus shows them (and us) that it is the hated outsider, the sinful Samaritan ("unclean" in religious terms because of his racial and ethnic heritage), who is, in the end, most faithful to what the law ultimately commands. Jesus doesn't debate this Scripture scholar on biblical terms. Instead, he points to a simple act of compassion as a living witness to everything Scripture intends to teach. Jesus leaves the Bible teacher (the lawyer) nearly speechless. The young man came to test the orthodoxy of Jesus, but leaves profoundly shaken, and likely more determined than ever to rid Israel of the menace of Jesus' teaching.

42. This story of the way Jesus handled Scripture made me wonder if our interpretive habits needed to be evangelized— that is, converted to the way of Jesus rather than the way many pastors and Bible teachers have handled Scripture over the centuries. If we take Jesus seriously, biblical fidelity must focus those of us who seek to live the truth of the Bible, not merely on the text of Scripture, but on its spirit. Discerning the spirit of Scripture requires more of us than simply saying,

"The Bible says it, I believe it, that settles it." That may be the way the young lawyer and many of the Pharisees of his day approached their Scriptures, but it's clearly not the way Jesus approached them.

43. So, while the Reformation cry "Scripture alone" was an important correction to many of the abuses of church authority growing out of the Middle Ages, it is clearly not enough to merely read the "letter of the law." We must interpret it wisely, allowing the living and active Word of God, the Lord Jesus Christ, who is "sharper than any two-edged sword," to cut away what is false from what is true (Heb 4:12). And if it is Jesus whom we follow, the result could likely be quite surprising to religious people.

44. In order to study the way in which the church of the past has handled controversy throughout history, seeking to give the living and active Word of God freedom to lead the church into faithfulness, our congregation also studied a series of historical controversies and explored the interpretive maneuvers involved in each of them. We observed the way not only the life of prayer and worship nourished the church with necessary wisdom during the challenges that came its way, but also the "life of the mind," and particularly the use of reason. There is a great intellectual tradition that informed the church's theological and ethical reflection about the new issues confronting Christians over time. The church in every age has found itself challenged to think, evaluate, understand, and make judgments through the art of logic, even when that logic wasn't evident to all. It is to a review of history and the role of human reason that we must now turn.

3

Why We Need History
and Reason

45. Christianity is a historical faith—that is, God not only entered history in Jesus Christ, but the Bible itself is a witness that God is revealed through historical events, persons, and experiences. We've all heard the obvious truth that those who do not understand or appreciate history are doomed to repeat its errors. So Christian faithfulness requires us to take history seriously.

46. God has given us minds to think. That doesn't mean we always use them well. Nor does it mean that one mind will necessarily understand another. But we are nevertheless called by God to use them to the best of our abilities (Rom 12:2). Yet there is always a higher authority than our minds. "Take every thought captive to obey Christ," said Saint Paul (2 Cor 10:5). We are to have "the mind of Christ" (1 Cor 2:16). Having the mind of Christ is more than simply repeating Scripture texts. Saint Paul's letters aren't merely a recitation of scriptural texts. The Jewish scribes often did

that; the early Christians did not. The living experience of the disciples with the Word of God himself, Jesus Christ, was their supreme guide. The story of Jesus' meeting with the two disciples on the Emmaus Road (Luke 24) is an example of the way minds can remain closed to the truth of the gospel even when they are looking hard at biblical texts. But through baptism, minds and hearts are opened, and we receive the anointing that can lead us into the truth (John 16:13). "His anointing teaches you about all things," taught Saint John. Though the early church's interpretation of Israel's Scriptures was different from Israel's religious tradition, John affirms that it "is true and is not a lie" (1 John 2:26–27). The Spirit of Jesus was the assurance within the disciple community that they would learn to interpret Scripture as Jesus did and not as the scribes and Pharisees of the Jews. True, the disciples' interpretations would often get them into trouble with the guardians of the biblical tradition, but as with Jesus, so it would be with his disciples. Jesus was very clear that obedience to the Spirit, not adherence to Israel's Scripture, would lead them into truth (John 16:12–15). But he was also clear about the consequences—persecution (John 16:1–4).

47. Obviously, this can be a dangerous teaching. We are rightly concerned about a kind of subjectivism that can justify anything. Scripture in our Reformed tradition is a critically important matter. But faithful *Christian* interpretation is an artful dance between our sacred texts, Jesus as revealed in those texts, history, the cultural context we find ourselves in, our own experience, and the presence and guidance of the Holy Spirit. We can't have Jesus without the Bible, but without Jesus, the Bible is unable to carry us into the fullness of what God intends for the world (John 5:39–40). This is where history and the use of reason are essential for

Christian faithfulness. "Jesus Christ, as he is attested to us in Holy Scripture," states the Barmen Declaration, "is the one Word of God whom we have to hear, and whom we have to trust and obey in life and in death."[1] This obedience is won by the hard work of informing our reason by revelation, and by using our reason to discern from history the unending testimony to God's presence among us and God's will for all creation. History shows us plenty of examples of both our fidelity and failure to live the way of God revealed in Jesus. This is why my own tribe, the Presbyterians, are confessional—we, for example, live under the authority of Holy Scripture and are guided by historical confessions of faith. The confessions were written at certain seasons in history when our faith needed to be summarized and interpreted again in moments of controversy and crisis. A faith that rests only on the Bible and refuses to use reason to evaluate the way the Bible has been interpreted and misinterpreted in history is, as we've heard before, doomed to repeat the errors of history.

48. So, as part of our congregation's study, "The Bible and Homosexuality," we not only examined the relevant parts of the Bible, we also explored case studies from church history that we believed could shed light on the mistakes and successes of the past two thousand years. We looked, for example, at Christology (what the church has come to believe about the person and work of Christ), as well as a number of other issues, scientific and social, that have confronted the church from time to time.

---

1. The Barmen Declaration (Germany, 1934) was a theological warning and protest written by a group of church leaders to help Christians understand the dangers of the Nazi heresies.

49. As I suggested at the beginning of this essay, we found that the church has made major changes in what it believes about Jesus Christ, the nature of the planet and its place in the solar system, the practice of slavery, and the role and authority of women in the church. We also found that most of the time these changes were initially violently opposed by the church but are now commonplace—nearly universally accepted.

50. What we believe about Jesus Christ, for example, was hotly contested during the early centuries of Christianity. The position most Christians today hold is not what much of the church believed in its early years. Through a simple appeal to Scripture, it was hard to argue that Christ is, as the Creed confesses, a full member of the Trinity, and is "the only Son of God, eternally begotten of the Father, God from God, Light from Light, true God from true God, begotten, not made, of one Being with the Father" through whom "all things were made" (Nicene Creed, 325 CE). It took more than 125 years and four ecumenical councils to arrive at this position. We learned that Arius (250–336 CE) was an Egyptian priest who was a literalist when it came to the Bible's teaching about the supremacy of God, and he was zealous for the Ten Commandments. Persuasively, Arius argued that the monotheism of Deuteronomy 6:4 is fundamental to Christian faith: "The Lord is our God, the Lord is one." He also argued that monotheism must be Christianity's essential witness against the paganism of the Roman Empire. With a simple appeal to biblical logic, he argued that in order to make sense of the Bible's prohibition against idolatry, the Son could not be of the same nature as the Father, but was created out of nothing. For if the Son was uncreated and of the same nature as the Father, then we would have two gods, not one.

And this was against the clear teaching of Holy Scripture. Among the texts he cited were Proverbs 8:22 and John 14:28. Without an appeal to the larger sense of the New Testament's witness, his logic was hard to deny. For many years, much of the church followed Arius—Jesus Christ was not divine.

51. Here's an aside. I realize that for some, this historical sketch may be tedious. Some of our people felt the same way. But for many in our congregation, it was enlightening. Never before had they taken time to understand the way the church has wrestled for truth over the ages. So, hang in there—I'm carrying you into the past so that you, too, can have a solid foundation for understanding our present conflict over an important issue and find a way into God's future.

52. Back to the argument. The journey of the church to its present and nearly universal understanding of the person and nature of Christ is a remarkable one, full of intrigue, twists, and turns. And it's instructive. The Nicene Creed, and its confession of the full divinity and humanity of Jesus Christ, was presented and debated at the first ecumenical council that met under the authority of Emperor Constantine in a city called Nicaea in Bithynia (not far from Constantinople/Byzantium/Istanbul). But the theology of that creed was not universally accepted throughout the empire. It wasn't until 381, at the Council of Constantinople, that a new emperor, Theodosius I, brought together both sides of the controversy and, through more struggle, eventually handed us the statement that now holds the church together with a theology that was once dismissed as unorthodox by the larger church: Jesus Christ is "the only Son of God, eternally begotten of the Father, God from God, Light from Light, true God from

true God, begotten, not made, of one Being with the Father," through whom "all things were made."

53. Having studied this history in light of the controversy now facing the church, we realized that much of what we now hold to be true was once thought to be heresy, and the process of coming to that universal, saving truth was messy. Of the Council of Constantinople in 381 (over seventy-five years after the first great debate), the church historian, Socrates Scholasticus, said: "The situation was exactly like a battle at night, for both parties seemed to be in the dark about the grounds on which they were hurling abuse at each other."[2] Theodosius did broker some kind of deal between warring parties that tilted in favor of our orthodox position today, but even then it was not finally and officially accepted by the whole church until the Council of Chalcedon in 451.

54. As we as a congregation faced this struggle about what the Bible says about homosexuality, it helped us to realize that Arius and his followers were serious about the Bible. But we also realized that the Bible alone is not enough. We must know how to interpret it. And we cannot interpret it alone. We must have conflict and challenge to move past our biases. This case taught us that it is possible to read the Bible seriously and miss Jesus Christ—as Arius did. It also taught us that minority opinions can be the right opinions in the long run, and that it may take many years for that to be made clear. This study also helped us realize that it's often unhelpful when dissenting groups break away from the larger church in favor of purity or like-mindedness. History teaches us that without the conflict necessary to come to the

2. Quoted in Rogers, *Presbyterian Creeds*, 48.

truth, we will often interpret the Bible myopically—that is, with narrow and defective vision.

55. The fact that minority opinions can often be right opinions and eventually be adopted by a majority of Christians became clear to us in another case. In the sixteenth century, the Renaissance mathematician and astronomer Nicholas Copernicus argued that the sun, not the earth, was the center of our solar system. Martin Luther denounced Copernicus as a "fool," saying, "This is what that fellow does who wishes to turn the whole of astronomy upside down." Then quoting Joshua 10:13, Luther said, "I believe the Holy Scriptures—for Joshua commanded the sun to stand still and not the earth."[3] To Luther, the Bible clearly taught that the earth, not the sun, stood at the center. Other prominent theologians and church officials joined in, dismissing Copernicus as an unfaithful innovator and heretic. Finally, in 1633 Galileo himself was tried and found guilty of heresy for following and promoting Copernicus's "errors." But as we all know, over time the weight of scientific evidence was too much for the church; it could no longer maintain its rigid recitation of biblical texts and instead recognized that the Bible doesn't give final and complete answers to everything. It points the way to truth, a truth fulfilled in Jesus Christ.

56. Grasping that truth, or rather, being grasped by it, requires a living relationship with the Author of the Bible, who alone can lead us into truths we may not yet see. It also requires that we stay in dialogue with those with whom we disagree, remaining curious without compromising the way we see things. And it takes time. Gobs of time. Time is our ally in the journey toward truth. Some fear that an appeal to

3. Kobe, "Copernicus and Martin Luther," 190.

time and patience is compromise. They worry that when it comes to sexual ethics, delays endanger young people who will be led astray from the Bible's teaching about sexuality, marriage, and identity, and, misled, these young people will shipwreck their lives. I think this kind of worry is actually dangerous. It's this kind of worry that forced Luther, for example, to make rash and unhelpful judgments about Copernicus—statements that in the long run made Christianity appear backward, foolish, and often pathetic in the eyes of those who often see truth before the church does. What young people today need is authentic, curious, and thoughtful engagement with the issues of the day. This is what will help them see the relevance of Jesus Christ for their lives. Obstructing an honest search for truth will not.

57. There are times, however, when patience and dialogue do endanger human life. And so, it takes an artful dance to know when to appeal to patience and when to push forward with single-minded determination. In the eighteenth century, Christians like John Newton and William Wilberforce viewed an appeal to patient reflection on the slave trade, and the use of the Bible to justify it, as an unacceptable delay.[4] The Atlantic was then heavily trafficked by ships, laden with human cargo—people packed into the bellies of vessels like sardines, bound from Africa to the New World. Many slaves perished en route. Those who didn't were destined for a life of servitude far from home, with no chance for freedom or dignity. These were human beings, made in the image of God, argued Wilberforce. But his arguments against the slave trade had scanty biblical support. Slave owners in Virginia

4. John Newton (1725–1807), onetime captain of a slave ship, became an evangelical Anglican minister; he also wrote the hymn "Amazing Grace." William Wilberforce (1759–1833) was an English politician and voice of the movement for the abolition of the slave trade.

and slave traders in London argued persuasively from the Bible in support of a thriving business practice.

58. I was in seminary when I learned how easy it is to use the Bible to support what history and reason have helped us realize is contrary to God's vision for the world. To drive this lesson home, Dr. Ron White, my "Presbyterian History and Creeds" professor, once divided up the class into two groups—one that would argue from the Bible *against* slavery, and the other that would use the Bible to argue *for* the practice of slavery. I was in the first group. We lost. Using biblical texts alone in order to argue against slavery was a daunting task. And our theological/ethical reflections made us appear soft on the Bible, like we didn't take it as seriously as our opponents did. After all, there are a number of biblical passages that clearly support slavery.[5] Leviticus 25:45 says, "You may also acquire them [slaves] from among the aliens residing with you, and from their families that are with you, who have been born in your land; and they may be your property." And Saint Paul teaches: "Let each of you remain in the condition in which you were called. Were you a slave when called? Do not be concerned about it" (1 Cor 7:20–21). The weight of Scripture is clearly in favor of a practice that the modern world has universally condemned—including some of the most conservative Christians who take the Bible quite literally.[6]

5. Genesis 17:2, Deuteronomy 20:10–11, Ephesians 6:1–5, Colossians 3:18–25 and 4:1, 1 Timothy 6:1–2, and the Letter to Philemon were all used to promote the slave trade as unassailably biblical. Slavery was practiced by the Hebrews as mandated by God. Further, Jesus never said a word against slaveholding. Even Saint Paul instructed an escaped slave, Onesimus, to return to his master.

6. To point out the hypocrisy of so many pro-slavery Christians in the nineteenth century, Abraham Lincoln once quipped: "Although volume upon volume is written to prove slavery is a very good thing, we never hear of the

59. As we worked through history, our congregation began to see that the same problems came into play regarding the historical role and authority of women in the church. The Old Testament is clear about the status of women. Men rule. Women were incredible vulnerable in the society shaped by the Old Testament; Deuteronomy 22:13–21, for example, reveals the incredible inequities and injustices women faced compared to men. And certain passages from Saint Paul's writing seem to follow suit. A woman must not teach a man, for she was deceived by the serpent and led Adam into sin (1 Tim 2:11–15). Women are to remain silent in public and must practice submission to men who hold headship over them (1 Cor 14:34–35). And while there are texts that seem to offer some confusing openness to the role of women in the early church (Rom 16), a literal reading of the Paul's writings can lead to the conclusion that the vocal role of women leaders in today's church and society is an aberration and contrary to the clear teaching of Scripture. But there are very few churches today, even the most conservative ones, that require the silence of their women in public.

60. A review of some of these key epochs in Christian history and the trajectory of the church's evolution made many of us wonder how it could be that the church, by and large, has come to accept things like the modern view of the cosmos, the evils of slavery, and the gifts of women to church and society when they are diametrically opposed to the views of the biblical writers.

---

man who wishes to take the good of it by being a slave himself." See The Gilder Lehrman Institute, "Lincoln Speech."

61. The truth is, the Bible doesn't give us the final answer on many things. The Bible is *authoritative,* which comes from the Latin *auctor*—meaning "originator" or "promoter." This indicates that Holy Scripture is our source, the spring from which our faith flows. It's clear that none of the Bible's writers intended to address every matter that would come up. Jesus never wrote a book. Instead, he meant, as was prophesied about him, to put the law on our hearts (Jer 31:33–34), and he intended that the Spirit would lead us into all truth (John 16:12–15). That clear fact in the teaching of Jesus ought to make us pause when people too vehemently say, "But the Bible says!" Such an appeal can put us at odds with the way of Jesus and the early church, which believed that faithful discernment requires adherence to four things: the rule of faith (which in the early church was the brief outline of the Apostle's teaching); a commitment to community life; frequent holy communion; and a life of daily prayer (Acts 2:42).

62. Many people would like the Bible to be a rule book or policy manual. It seems that things would be much easier that way. And many have made it into one—contrary to its nature and purpose. Jesus certainly struggled against those in his day who tried to do just that with the Jewish Scriptures. But the fact is, a policy manual is not what God gave us when God gave us Jesus, the new Moses. A policy manual is not what the Bible is. Policies are policies because they make things utterly clear, less open to interpretation; they create nonnegotiable standards. Christians look to the Bible as a witness to Jesus Christ, a guide for understanding what God is up to in Christ, and how we live in light of that revelation. The Bible is not a policy manual. And so, there's a freedom to faithful Christian interpretation of the Bible. It's grounded in the authority and sufficiency of Christ, and in relation to

the presence of the Holy Spirit. Frankly, that can feel awfully squishy for some people. But that way of relating to the Bible is the way of Jesus, like it or not. And it's this liberated, live-by-the-Spirit-not-the-law kind of religion (Gal 5:16) that got Saint Paul into such trouble with those who wanted more certainty, clearer rules.

63. There are other religions that offer a greater degree of certitude about their book and more rules for living a religious life than Christianity does. Christianity is about a living Word, Jesus Christ. And the Bible directs us to him; it's essentially *instrumental*—that is, it is not an end in itself; rather, it's a means to an end. That end is obedience to Jesus Christ, who "is the one Word of God whom we have to hear, and whom we have to trust and obey in life and in death" (The Barmen Declaration). Of course, that leaves the church open to mistakes as it seeks to live in obedience to this living Word. It's clear from history that mistakes happen and will happen again. This is why we must be students of history and offer our minds to Jesus Christ (Rom 12:2), taking every thought captive to Jesus Christ (2 Cor 10:5), so that by reasoning together—guided by Scripture, our confessional history,[7] a life of prayer, strengthened by the sacraments, and our missional involvement in the world—we may discern the way the One who is "the way, the truth, and the life" (John 14:6) is leading us to live out the gospel today.

64. As we, in our congregation, worked through this history of Christianity's reasoned engagement with the Bible and the challenges that inevitably came at the church, many of

7. For Presbyterians in particular, this means allowing ourselves to be guided by the major theological statements the church has made over time. These statements, or confessions, appear in our *Book of Confessions*, Part One of The Constitution of the Presbyterian Church (U.S.A.).

us became uncomfortable. Many of us wanted more clarity, not less. Today's world worries us. We look around and see problems everywhere. And there *are* plenty of problems, to be sure. Many Christians see what's happening around them—the moral decadence, the relativism, the loss of faith in organized religion—and they worry that the church is following a godless culture, not leading it into the holiness of God. But I find this too pessimistic; this worry seems too willing to see the absence of God rather than the presence of God. And a view of the absence of God in the world, no matter how challenging things become, doesn't square with the witness of the Bible and history.

65. Scripture teaches that creation is never devoid of the presence of God, never without the power of the One who brought it into being and is bringing all things to reconciled fullness in Christ (Col 1:15–20). "The whole earth is full of God's glory," declared Isaiah (6:3). And the Holy Spirit was often out in front of God's people, "doing a new thing" (Isa 43:16), revealing the will of God outside the church before the church itself was able to see the "new thing" God intended to do (Acts 10). History shows this to be true as well. The Holy Spirit has often been out in front of the church, inviting it forward, urging it to change and grow. The cases I've presented above are examples of just this kind of holy pressure coming toward the church by the Spirit from outside the church.

66. All this made me seriously consider the possibility that the God whose mission it is "to gather up all things in Christ" (Eph 1:10) was moving again upon the church from the outside. I wondered if it is possible that God is once again inviting the church to overturn old opinions and positions,

this time about human sexuality—opinions and positions that have long vilified and injured children of God who have been excluded from the church and God's gospel because of an orientation that is, scientifically, part of their biological identity.[8]

67. All that I've explored here does not necessarily mean that God is overturning old opinion and positions. In fact, what I've explored about Scripture and history so far in this essay was not enough to push me over the old line in the sand, and toward embracing what I now believe is the will of God—to include gay and lesbians fully in the life of the church and gospel. But it was enough to open me to the possibility. It is the pastoral and missional situation facing the church, as well as what I call the trajectory of the Greatest Command-ment and the new creation, that finally moved me toward a full embrace of the gospel of inclusion. I now believe that, just as in the past, God is raising up a new generation of re-formers who, though their vision will be rejected and resist-ed by some, are led by God to guide the church and society through yet another change. We can already look backward with gratitude because we no longer believe that the earth is the center of the universe. We are grateful that we no longer believe it's a good and just thing to enslave human beings for economic gain. Millions of us across the planet are grateful that our children, both boys and girls, are growing up with a very different understanding of the relationships between men and women because we no longer believe that women are inferior to men, required to remain silent and submis-sive in church and society. One day, we will look back with

8. This statement is, of course, hotly contested in some religious circles. The religious resistance today to this fact appears to me to be very similar to the religious resistance to the findings of Copernicus and Galileo centuries ago.

gratitude because we have stepped across another threshold of injustice and we no longer believe that gay and lesbian persons are depraved; we no longer believe that their desire for safety, security, and stability within marriage and family life must be sublimated; and we no longer believe that their expressions of love are criminal acts.

68. But I'm getting ahead of myself and the story I'm telling. I must now turn to the two final developments in my journey toward an understanding of the gospel that views the full inclusion of gays and lesbians as a necessary implication of the truth that those "who once were far off have been brought near by the blood of Christ" (Eph 2:13).

4

The Pastoral and Missional Situation

69. Saul, the Pharisee, was dead set on exterminating the troublesome sect of Christ followers until his life was fully reoriented to the gospel through a personal encounter, first with the Lord Jesus, and then with those he'd set out to destroy. He was certain that his religious viewpoint was right and that the views of the followers of Jesus were wrong—dangerously wrong. But a meeting with the Risen Christ on the road to Damascus proved to him that his entrenched viewpoint kept him blind to the revelation of God through Jesus Christ. Then followed a meeting with the disciples of Jesus he'd labeled as heretics and apostates. To his surprise, he found they were not only the ones who saw the true light of God, but that he needed them to help him see what he'd been missing (Acts 9:1–31). On the heels of Saul's conversion, Luke tells us of a similar transformation in Peter's vision. Through personal encounter with a feared, hated, and religiously unclean Roman warrior, Peter is led by God to confess: "I truly understand that God shows no partiality,

but in every nation anyone who fears him and does what is right is acceptable to him" (Acts 10:34–35).

70. The same is true throughout history. Personal encounter is the opener of eyes. It's easy to judge and exclude from a distance. But when William Wilberforce, for example, personally encountered African slaves and saw the light of God in their eyes, he could no longer believe the rhetoric that advanced the cause of slavery and injustice. These were human beings with souls, made in the image of God. That encounter led to the dismantling of what nearly all people today acknowledge as a terrible evil, sustained too long by religious dogma and blindness to the true trajectory of the gospel. Of Wilberforce, Eric Metaxas writes:

> Wilberforce overturned not just European civilization's view of slavery but its view of almost everything in the human sphere; and that is why it's nearly impossible to do justice to the enormity of his accomplishment: it was nothing less than a fundamental and important shift in human consciousness.
>
> In typically humble fashion, Wilberforce would have been the first to insist that he had little to do with any of it. The facts are that in 1785, at age twenty-six and at the height of his political career, something profound and dramatic happened to him. He might say that, almost against his will, God opened his eyes and showed him another world. Somehow Wilberforce saw God's reality—what Jesus called the Kingdom of Heaven. He saw things he had never seen before, things that we quite take for granted today but that were as foreign to his world as slavery is to ours. He saw things that existed in God's reality but that, in human reality, were nowhere in evidence. He saw the idea that all men and women are created equal by God, in his image, and are therefore sacred.[1]

1. NPR, "'Amazing Grace' and the End of the Slave Trade."

71. In the winter of 2008 a pastor called me. He was frantic. His college-age son had just come out to the family and they were in a free fall with no one to turn to. There are very few resources in the church for this kind of experience and it turns the world upside down for religious families. The loneliness these families and their children face is intense. There are no support groups, few books, no one else in the church wearing a sign that says "I have a gay kid." But there is a lot of fear and isolation from the very resources that ought to sustain such families plunged into a suffocating darkness. They are suddenly thrown into a world they know very little about, a world they did not choose to enter, but one they cannot escape.

72. These families, like their children, need pastoral care. They need the gospel, and they need a community that knows what it means to live the gospel. But, unlike the pastor who called me in the winter of 2008, very few of them turn to the church. Most of them live in fear of judgment, alienation, and gossip. The very communities that are created by the Lord Jesus as places free from shame are those that keep people chained to it. Consequently many Christian parents deny the reality of what their child has told them, and this plunges them into a whole new experience of relational trauma. I've counseled young people whose Christian families have utterly rejected them, and I've counseled those whose families have done their best to go on loving and supporting them. The truth is, both the gay person and his or her family now live in a world they've had no preparation for. One father once told me through tears, "Before I knew my son was gay, my biggest fears on a Friday night were that

43

he'd get drunk, get someone pregnant, or wreck the car. But in this city I now worry that he won't come home *alive*."

73. And then, what of the gay person herself or himself? The church has clearly been inhospitable to those who come to realize they don't fit the mold of traditional heterosexual courtship and marriage. There is no place for them and there are no socializing forces to guide them. Left to themselves, to the Internet, or to the often aberrant versions of human community in the clubs and bars clustered in gay ghettos across America, they must navigate the challenging gauntlet of human sexuality. Doing so is hard enough for heterosexual kids with ample models and resources, but those without them must walk alone, and if not alone they often consort with those who are themselves deeply wounded and are too often unsavory guides. The result is a higher than normal incidence of self-abuse, self-hatred, substance abuse, flagrant promiscuity, and feelings of being despised by God and rejected by those who ought to love them. Such isolation often leads to depression, and depression leads to a high incidence of suicide among gay and lesbian young people.[2]

74. All of us today know people whose sexual orientation differs from what we've considered normative for most of history. Increasingly, we are coming to learn that homosexual people simply want the same things heterosexual people want. We know gay and lesbian persons (bisexual and transgender persons, too) not as abominations and so-called perverts, but as the neighbor who brought food after a loved one died, the teacher who helped our ADHD daughter feel successful, the student who hung around our classroom

2. The recent "It Gets Better" campaign is a valiant effort to turn the tide of despair, depression, and suicide among gay youth.

because he was afraid to go home at the end of the day, the accountant who helped us sort through business options when the recession nearly ruined us, or the veterinarian whose shoulder we cried on when we had to put our dog down. Maybe she's the cop who keeps our neighborhood safe, the mechanic who works on our car. The bottom line is, gay people are our children, our parents, our siblings, our favorite aunt, a neighbor, coworker, or friend. We all have personal encounters with gay people, and those encounters are more frequent than we realize.

75. Frankly, it's the personal reality of homosexuality that's forcing many of us to listen again for what Scripture teaches, and to examine the ways the church has, throughout history, handled the kinds of controversies I've explored above. When real people we care about are maligned and discriminated against, suffering for a sexual orientation they did not choose, we ask new questions. Christians did this at each stage of our history when new controversies challenged the faith. And in each of the examples I cited in the previous section, the church, by and large, emerged with new answers—firmly grounded in Scripture and tradition—that have become the norm today, despite the fact that they were nearly unimaginable prior to the struggle.

76. This is the way a truly *evangelical* theology is hammered out. It is formed and reformed on the anvil of real life. No ivory-tower dogma will work for a gospel-centered Christianity. An evangelical theology that is truly good news and worthy of Jesus Christ must address the lives of real people pastorally; it doesn't dabble in abstractions, it doesn't pretend to be objective. Why? Because there's there's nothing objective and abstract about the incarnation of God. In Jesus

Christ, God gets close and personal, subject to the complexities of our humanity. And that subjectivity, that closeness, has changed everything.

77. Take Saint Paul, for example. Without a personal encounter with God and with those God sent to show him the way of the gospel, he would have kept killing Christians rather than becoming the fiercest advocate for the universal relevance of Jesus Christ for all people—Jew and Gentile, man and woman, Greek and non-Greek, and so on (see Acts 9). Similarly, Saint Peter was converted to Christ's way of inclusion for the despised Romans who the Holy Spirit was drawing into the family of God (see Acts 10). So it's consistent with a gospel-immersed Christianity for us to welcome relationships that will affect and change our theology. Relationships—messy, challenging, and bewildering—open our eyes and our hearts to discern the true path of the gospel in our world, a path that will require us to change because of the relationships we're involved in.

78. Since that pastor called me in the winter of 2008 and drew me into the storm of his family's life, more than a dozen gay young adults have come out to me. I've also tried to gather together the dozens of families in our church who have gay sons or daughters. The families of gay children often feel more alone and without guidance than do their children. Gay kids at least can find LGBT communities, but there are no parents-of-gay-kids parts of town for parents to go to for support. Yet gay persons and their families need not be so alone. If you get to know gay people and learn of the trouble they have trying to find their bearings in their families, schools, and workplaces, you'll come face-to-face with the massive challenges before them. And what you learn will

humanize those who have been dehumanized for too long; you'll find they're a lot like you. That pastor's gay son, for example, told me that all he wanted was "to have a good marriage like my parents."

79. The point is, you never really know whether or not someone you're living or working with may be living with a secret they've never found the courage to tell you about. I myself have two gay sons. One came out to me when he was sixteen. The other told me in his early twenties. They're remarkable adults. Bright. Handsome. Socially engaged. Successful in their fields. In good relationships. They dispel all of the myths conservative religion likes to peddle about homosexual men. They are not effeminate. They were not raised without a strong masculine role model. Nor are they the product of an emotionally bottled-up, distant, or abusive father. No, they were made the way they are. And their lives have opened me and those who love them to the kind of gospel preached by Saint Paul, to the vision glimpsed by Saint Peter, who said, "I truly understand that God shows no partiality" (Acts 10:34). These relationships have opened my eyes to see the height, breadth, length, and depth of the gospel's reach.

80. Things change when someone you care for deeply tells you they're gay. In fact, I find it's quite difficult to have a meaningful conversation about God, the Bible, and homosexuality with someone who *doesn't* have a real relationship with a gay or lesbian person. Unless they've heard the stories of gays and lesbians and their families, and can feel some compassion for their experience—even if they can't, in good conscience, accept it—it's too easy for people to talk abstractly about homosexuality as an "issue" confronting church and society. These are *persons*, and when we get

personally involved, we can no longer tell ourselves there's such a thing as an "objective theology." Saint Peter's theology was changed—or better, evangelized—by the Holy Spirit when he was sent by God to the house of a Roman centurion. When he stepped over the threshold of a Roman house—making himself ritually unclean according to the laws and ordinances of his Jewish religion—he could no longer deny God's love for those he once dismissed. He was no longer "objective"—that is, distanced from personal involvement. The Roman military man's household was full of *persons* whom God loved, regardless of their race, ethnicity, religion, gender, age, or anything else. And in response to the revelation of God in Christ, who is always breaking down walls, Peter could only submit himself in humility to the evidence of God at work, gathering together what has too long been kept apart.

81. Now, finding out that I have two gay sons may lead some readers to dismiss what I'm saying here. They'll argue that my reading of the Bible and history isn't objective—that I'm too personally involved to seek the truth. Well, of course I'm not objective. No one is. The truth is, there's no such thing as an "objective theology." The things we seek to make sense of theologically are all personal and relational. You can't, for example, treat war as an abstraction if you've got a soldier in the family; you're personally involved. Gun control isn't a mere political debate if you've lost a child in a school shooting or if you're a hunter; you're personally involved. If you know the real stories of hardworking Mexican families who are separated by fences and laws, or have a relationship with the Muslim physician who lost a whole lot of suspicious patients after September 11, 2001, you'll have a very different take on immigration than you would have otherwise.

Conversely, you can take a hard line against abortion when you're not personally involved, if you're unaffected by that reality. But things change when your daughter's been raped and now carries a child that reminds her, and you, of the nightmare you all now live with on a daily basis.

82. And so, when homosexuality becomes personal, it's no longer an abstract concept we can debate with distanced objectivity. Our words and ideas have consequences for real people we care about. When we know real people who have too long been dismissed and even demonized, we, like so many who've gone before us and who faced other controversies, will find ourselves shifting, our minds changing. Like William Wilberforce centuries ago, we will find ourselves stirred by the truth that confronted him when the evils of the slave trade became deeply personal: "all men and women are created equal by God, in his image, and are therefore sacred." We will come to realize that excluding people because of their sexual orientation is an injustice we can no longer tolerate. This is what has happened to me and is happening to many people around me. And it's not a cave-in to a culture of moral expediency as I've heard many people say. It's a thoughtful reengagement with evangelical theology by faithful people who are doing the same thing other Christians did at other times in our history.

83. The pastoral and personal context, combined with the biblical survey above, provide a compelling argument for a reconsideration of the church's historical stance against all same-sex relationships. But in my mind, there is one more reality—the missional context—that shifts the momentum dramatically toward a mandate for change.

84. In 2007, the Barna Group published a report entitled, "A New Generation Expresses Its Skepticism and Frustration with Christianity."[3] The report showed that in 2007 only 16 percent of 16- to 29-year-olds had a favorable opinion of the church. The rest said "no thanks." Eighty-seven percent said the church is too judgmental. Eighty-five percent said it is hypocritical. Seventy-eight percent said it is old-fashioned. Seventy-five percent said it is too involved in conservative politics. Seventy percent said it is insensitive to those who are different. Sixty-eight percent said it is boring. And 64 percent said it is not accepting of people of other faiths. But above all, consider this:

> Today, the most common perception [among young people] is that present-day Christianity is 'anti-homosexual.' Overall, 91% of young non-Christians and 80% of young churchgoers say this phrase describes Christianity. As the research probed this perception, non-Christians and Christians explained that beyond their recognition that Christians oppose homosexuality, they believe that Christians show excessive contempt and unloving attitudes towards gays and lesbians.

85. These statistics are dated now, but they reveal an alarming trajectory, and it's unlikely that the trend has reversed or even slowed down. In fact, recently, the Barna Group reported that nearly 60 percent of the young people who are raised in the church will walk away from it.[4] And, in an extensive learning project, the Barna Group invites the church to take seriously the question, "How can we reverse the trend?"[5]

3. Barna Group, "A New Generation Expression its Skepticism and Frustration with Christianity." See also David Kinnaman's *unChristian*.

4. Barna Group, "Six Reasons Young Christians Leave Church."

5. Barna Group, "How Can We Reverse the Trend?"

86. This is the kind of question that haunts a pastor and evangelist like me, and it raises important questions for the leaders of my congregation. We believe the gospel of Jesus Christ is good news for all and that we must put no obstacle in anyone's way that would prevent them from receiving an unmistakable and unqualified invitation to embrace the love of God in Christ (2 Cor 6:1–10). If young Americans were an unreached tribe, one we were seriously failing to reach, wouldn't we reevaluate our mission strategy? Wouldn't we listen to this tribe's people, exploring their way of life, looking for ways the gospel is calling us to change just as much as it's calling them to change? Wouldn't we also expose the unnecessary roadblocks between them and the fullness of life they seek but cannot find elsewhere? And wouldn't we ask, as any missiologist worth his or her salt would ask, what can we learn about the gospel from this tribe? Vincent Donovan did this among the Masai of East Africa. Don and Carol Richardson did the same among the Sawi peoples of New Guinea. Some missionaries, on the other hand, once thought that the Christian missionary task in Africa was to create black Europeans. There were Scottish Presbyterian missionaries who tried to create a Sudanese tribesman who could walk and talk and think like a Scottish Presbyterian. So they imported pipe organs and hymnals from Europe to Khartoum, Sudan, and ignored the need for the Dinka tribe to sing God's praise with drums and rattles and dancing. The truth is, mission is not about passing on our expressions as the norm, but about inviting others to embrace the faith through their own cultural expressions. The best European missionaries understood that mission was not about en-culturation, but about contextualization—that is, letting go of the gospel so the gospel itself could give birth to a truly

African Christianity, quite possibly looking very different from its European parentage.

87. American culture is changing rapidly. For some religious people that's a frightening reality. They wring their hands and lament these changes, arguing that we must take America back for Christ. They worry that Christianity is becoming too much like the culture around it, floating along blindly amid the flotsam of this broad river that's sweeping America into cultural and moral decay, and toward spiritual apostasy. They argue that the church is to lead culture, not follow it. But I find that argument strange and untenable for an evangelist. The Holy Spirit has always been out in front of a stubborn and often recalcitrant church, inviting it into God's future. When it's been most vibrant, most spiritually potent, the church has never believed that the church is the only place where God is active in the world. To argue that is to misread not only history but also Scripture. The world, the Bible says, is not devoid of God or even thin on God's presence. Rather, "the whole earth is full of God's glory" (Isa 6:3). A church that circles the wagons is a broken church. A Christianity that closes its ears to outside voices is a church deaf to the invitation of God, resistant to the Holy Spirit's pull. If a truly African Christianity required European and American missionaries to relinquish the gospel and give it freedom within African culture so that it could truly flourish there, so too we who have held to an older moral vision for sexuality need to relinquish the gospel to the younger generations if the gospel is to find a home among them and carry the church into the twenty-first century. Doing so may be frightening to us, that's true. But not doing so is dangerous to the gospel. It keeps the gospel too tightly held and controlled by those who are in power.

88. Recently, Pope Francis, known as a conservative theologically, and passionate about Jesus evangelistically, has pushed the Roman Catholic Church toward greater openness to the world. In the first major statement of this vision, "The Joy of the Gospel," the pope calls the church to emerge from itself and penetrate the various peripheries of the world. "All of us are called to take part in this new missionary 'going forth,'" he writes. "Each Christian and every community must discern the path that the Lord points out, but all of us are asked to obey his call to go forth from our own comfort zone in order to reach all the 'peripheries' in need of the light of the Gospel."[6] When the church is too preoccupied with self-preservation, he said, it becomes narcissistic. In fact, the Roman Church made huge strides as a faith unafraid of the world under Pope John XIII and through the reforms of Vatican II. Vatican II ushered in a vibrant era of the church's life—it was followed by explosive growth and engagement with world religions, politics, and social issues without losing its core convictions. But under the more recent popes, it began to withdraw, draw tighter lines, and became, in this new pope's mind, repressive and self-absorbed. And because of that, it has suffered. Because Pope Francis is conservative—that is, passionate about Jesus—he is therefore more willing to follow him into the world, bringing new hope to much of the Catholic Church, and opening a new era of real engagement between the gospel and where people actually live.

89. In the same way, I believe we must learn from the shifts and changes in culture around us. We must listen for the Holy Spirit speaking to us through voices from beyond the

6. Pope Francis, "Apostolic Exhortation: Evangelii Gaudium [The Joy of the Gospel]," paragraph 20.

broken church; we must penetrate the periphery and listen, really listen. Might it be that young people today, so critical of the church, are a voice from God challenging us once again to change in order for us to more fully embody the gospel in our times? Might it be that as with cosmology at the time of Copernicus and Galileo, or as with slavery during Wilberforce's lifetime, the marginal voices are calling the church to change for the sake of Jesus' mission to gather in all people? Young people today will not be won to Christ and gathered into our communities of faith because we hold a traditional line on homosexuality. Instead, they will find themselves drawn to the Christ who welcomes the outsider, has compassion for the marginalized, and embraces those whom religious people have turned away. They are pointing us to the future of Christianity, and unless we change, we may well find ourselves opposing God (Acts 5:38). Opposing God is, unfortunately, not uncommon for religiously serious people. Unfortunately, it often takes far too long for them to learn from and acknowledge their mistakes.

Now let me summarize what I've said so far.

90. First, I've shown in chapters 1 and 2 above that while the biblical texts that speak directly about homosexuality cannot be used to advocate for the full inclusion of gay and lesbian persons in the church, they do not necessarily block the kind of change I've come to believe is necessary if we are to be faithful to Jesus Christ. Second, my review of Christian doctrinal and ethical history in chapter 3 provides testimony to the way Christians have changed their minds on a number of issues which the church once considered settled, and eventually embraced positions earlier Christians couldn't imagine tolerating. Third, in this chapter I've explored the experience

of real people we know and love, people who happen to be gay but who desire safe, secure, monogamous relationships. I've also surveyed the way a missional approach to culture invites us to reexamine our traditional beliefs. I believe pastoral and missional realities challenge us to reconsider the church's historic condemnation of homosexuality. Condemning homosexuality is pastorally disastrous to individuals and families, and disregards the missional realities facing the communication of the gospel today. Taken together, all that I've said so far may be persuasive to many readers. However, for me, though these are persuasive justifications for rethinking Christianity's position, they do not yet fully mandate the change I propose.

91. There is one final area of reflection that does. And that is what I will refer to as the outworking of Christ's "Greatest Commandment," and the New Testament's vision of the "new creation." To these twin pillars of evangelical faith I now turn.

5

The Trajectory of the Greatest Commandment and the New Creation

92. As my congregation and I walked this road together we kept ourselves fastened to Jesus Christ as the source, center, and future of the Christian faith. "I am the way and the truth and the life," said Jesus, "no one comes to the Father except by me" (John 14:6). We agreed that this does not dismiss the Hebrew Bible (the Old Testament), but our confession of Jesus Christ does mean that we need to read the Hebrew Scriptures with different eyes than our Jewish friends do. For us, the whole Bible points to Jesus Christ. It finds its fulfillment in the revelation of God in Christ, and cannot be read properly by Christians apart from reference to Christ. The story of the two disciples walking along the road to Emmaus on the evening of the first Easter is a good example of the way Christians learned to read the Old in light of the New: without Christ as the new and true interpreter, we are blind to what the Old Testament really intends (Luke 24:13–35).

93. The relationship between the two Testaments—between the law and the gospel, Judaism and Christianity—and the degree of continuity between them is a hotly debated and complex relationship. We struggled with this relationship, some of us falling in more with the law, while others leaned more fully toward the gospel. But we realized that we had to explore this relationship intelligently. We found that unless we critically examined our often-superficial approach to the relationship between law and gospel, Old and New, we would miss the trajectory of the Bible. In order to fully understand and appreciate the gospel we realized we needed to see that what biblical writers knew of God grew and changed over the course of the Bible's history. Malachi has a more expanded vision than that of Moses. And what Isaiah glimpsed becomes a full reality to John the evangelist. So, in order to understand what I say here, even if you might disagree with it, you need to take this journey too. Like my congregation, which looked deeply at these things, you also need to understand how and why Jesus and the writers of the New Testament had a very different relationship to the Hebrew Scriptures than did those who opposed them. Jesus Christ is the sole reason for this difference.

94. There is no question that the New Testament writers are absolutely preoccupied with Jesus Christ. They are bound to his singular vision of the Greatest Commandment: "You shall love the Lord your God with all your heart, and with all your soul, and with all your strength, and with all your mind; and your neighbor as yourself" (Luke 10:27). And they are enthralled by the implications of God's "new creation" in Christ—the reconciliation created through the event of Christ (2 Cor 5:11–21). In Galatians 6:15–16, Saint Paul says that "neither circumcision nor uncircumcision is anything,

but the new creation is everything!" For them and for us, the past is subservient to God's future (this, incidentally, is a key theme in the Letter to the Hebrews).

95. This doesn't mean that we ignore the past. No, without the past there would be no Christ as we know him. But we can't minimize the effects of the dramatic change that has come in and through Jesus Christ. This is a fact the New Testament makes clear. Some Christians treat the Old and New Testaments as if the New flows neatly, or seamlessly, from the Old. It does flow from the Old, but honestly, it doesn't flow neatly. Reading the two Testaments is like gliding down a river and then suddenly finding yourself turning an abrupt corner and heading into a long run of rapids, over a small waterfall, and then into a vast and glorious ocean. And where you end up is a lot bigger than where you started. This movement from small to large, particular to universal, the Alpha to the Omega is the trajectory of the Bible itself. It all starts in a garden and ends in a vast city. The event of Jesus Christ is like creation all over again, a new Big Bang. Explosive. Eruptive. In the dynamdic and expansive entrance of God in Jesus Christ, the reign of God has come among us to lead all creation toward its consummation.

96. The Old Testament isn't without hints at the coming change, the eruption of the reign of God. Isaiah foresaw it. He declared that God was coming to "do a new thing" (Isa 43:19), reversing the old order of brokenness and alienation, death and despair (65:17–25). What's more, he saw that even non-Jews as well as those previously excluded because of their sexual identity would be welcomed into the covenant community (56:3–5). Isaiah's was a daring vision, but it didn't come to pass until "in these last days [God spoke] to

us by a Son, whom he appointed heir of all things, through whom he also created the worlds" (Heb 1:2).

97. Our congregation studied and debated, and listened and learned in classes and groups. And in Sunday worship, I preached the New Testament readings from the Revised Common Lectionary. As I did, I felt like something new was happening to me. The New Testament was coming alive to me in fresh ways. As I read and preached from the apostles, they seemed nearly breathless with excitement as they reveled in the person and work of Jesus Christ. And Christ became bigger and better than anything I'd yet dared imagine. I also realized that the theological transition from the Hebrew to the Christian Scriptures was a tumultuous one; I sensed real tension in their writings as the theologians, pastors, and evangelists of the early church struggled to honor the Old while embracing the radical nature of the New. Reading the bold and visionary declarations about Jesus in the high Christological language of Ephesians, Philippians, and Colossians, I was struck by the shift in mood from the Hebrew books of the Bible to the Christian ones.

98. "It's little wonder," I thought to myself one day as I worked on a biblical text, "that the early Christian leaders, though mostly Jewish in background, had real trouble with their own people, the Jews." An honest reading of the New Testament showed me that the early Christians often seemed to play footloose and fancy free with the Hebrew Scriptures. They made audacious claims, taking things out of context, advocating what faithful Jews considered to be lunacy at best and heresy at worst. But the disciples of Jesus came by it honestly; Jesus did it too. That's one of the things that got him killed. What Jesus was teaching about the reign of God

wasn't obvious from a plain reading of Scripture. "If it was," a church member once asked me, "then why did the religious authorities fight against him? Their quarrel with Jesus only makes sense if what he said and did wasn't plain to everyone who heard the Scriptures read in synagogue each week. It had to be new and different for the religious teachers to become so enraged at him." She was right. This became clearer to me when I was preparing a sermon on Matthew 11. Reading Matthew, I realized that even Jesus' own cousin, John the Baptist, with whom Jesus had grown up, couldn't understand what he was up to. Jesus' agenda didn't square with what John read in the Hebrew Scriptures (see Matt 3:1–12 and 11:2–6). The fact is, both Jesus and his followers believed that having faith in the eruption of God's reign here and now required them to hold loosely to the Hebrew Scriptures—tethered to them, yes, but never merely repeating them. Something new was at hand. And because it was, whenever long-cherished biblical texts worked in contradiction with the compassion they saw and heard in Jesus, they minimized the importance of those texts or ignored them completely. Of course, the religious authorities weren't amused.

99. The fact is, Jesus preached the reign of God, not the law of Moses. He acknowledged the law, but never sat down like the scribes to study it. And he never required his disciples to study it. He didn't affirm it nor did he attack it. Instead, he often went beyond the law and prophetic writings, taking the supreme authority as the true interpreter of Scripture upon himself. Most of his hearers were, therefore, outraged (Luke 5:16–29). Reading the Gospels, I noticed that whenever Jesus talked religion, he didn't talk like the scribes and Pharisees who asked, "Is such and such in accordance with the law? Is it right or wrong according to Moses?" Instead, Jesus asked,

"Are God's people being helped or hurt?" I saw that the real lives of real people were his focus. He wasn't too concerned with maintaining the tradition or upholding the institution. In fact, he often subverted it. When he ran into sabbath laws that were hurting people, he broke them (e.g., Matt 12:1–8; Mark 3:1–6; Luke 13:10–17; 14:1–6; John 5:1–18; 9:1–40). He also transgressed the purity laws when they excluded people from the very religion that ought to have saved them (e.g., Matt 11:18–19; 15:1–20; Luke 8:22–56; 15:1–2; John 4:1–42; 8:1–11). Those who were wounded by religion were delighted by his flagrant disobedience to laws that marginalized them or held them captive. The pious were shocked. The religious authorities fumed and plotted his death.

100. All this rose up before me as if I was beholding a vast landscape in which a mighty river made a sweeping turn, fundamentally changing everything around it—like the great Colorado River carving a 180-degree turn in sheer rock at Horseshoe Bend in Arizona. When we enter the pages of the New Testament, there is this kind of massive energy carving a new direction in God's dealings with humanity and creation. The event of Jesus Christ changes everything. This is why we must be wary of those who say in the case of homosexuality that we must go backward into the Old Testament for our answers. Of course, the New Testament writers read the Old Testament. But they read it with new eyes—always focused on the new thing God is doing in Jesus Christ. They held the Old loosely, treasuring it without revering it in the same way they were coming to revere Jesus Christ, the living Word of God.

101. "Do not think I have come to abolish the law or the prophets," Jesus said. "I have come not to abolish but to

fulfill" (Matthew 5:17). There's honor and respect in the first half of his sentence, but in the second, he loosens his hearers from the law and makes the daring claim that the tradition is summed up in himself—that he is more important than the law and prophets (cf. Luke 4:16–21; John 5:39–42). In fact, he is the fulfillment of all the tradition's seeing and yearning. The Sermon on the Mount is Jesus' way of honoring the Old but going beyond its laws, ordinances, rituals, and moral codes. Instead, Jesus focuses on the heart of the matter. If the heart is pure, he says, the law of God is already at work apart from the external commands and ordinances. (Saint Paul will pick up this theme in his Letter to the Galatians.)

102. Jesus knew that anybody can obey a law. You can obey the law by not killing, but if you don't come to terms with the anger and jealousy and violence within your own heart, the law hasn't brought you close to God; it's only aligned you with an external code of ethics, and given you a tool by which you judge the outer behavior of others. Jesus says that kind of tool is not only worthless when it comes to your life with God, it's dangerous—to you and others. This is why Jesus blasts the biblically serious scribes and Pharisees, saying, "Woe to you, scribes and Pharisees, hypocrites! For you tithe mint, dill, and cumin, and have neglected the weightier matters of the law: justice and mercy and faith. It is these you ought to have practiced without neglecting the others. You blind guides! You strain out a gnat but swallow a camel" (Matt 23:23–24). It is the heart that matters to Jesus, and the only law that ultimately matters is the law of love. According to Jesus, the whole of the law can be practiced faithfully by living a life singularly devoted to loving God and loving your neighbor (Matt 22:34–40).

103. There is nothing greater than love. And, according to Jesus, the whole of biblical faith can be summed up in this singular law: the "law" of love. Love is the energy that flows within and from the three persons of the Trinity. Love is the source, substance, and goal of faith. Love is the one thing that will be left when we no longer "see" the goal of our faith "in a mirror, dimly," but finally see God "face to face" (1 Cor 13:8–13). Love is the motive of the incarnation, suffering, death, and resurrection of Jesus (John 3:16). Love is the motive of all Christian mission (2 Cor 5:14). Without love, no amount of fidelity to laws and ordinance, rituals, and moral codes means anything at all. Saint Paul, of course, says this beautifully in his summary of the Christian life in 1 Corinthians 13. Saint John also follows this trajectory in his teaching to the early Christians: "God is love," and the sole work of the Christian is to "abide in love" (1 John 4:16). "If we love one another, God dwells in us, and God's love is perfected in us" (1 John 4:7). And when you love, you abide in God, and "do not need anyone to teach you"—this anointing of love will teach you the way of truth and not of error (1 John 2:27). The most pious may achieve great religious status, but if their lives are devoid of love, their fidelity is nothing more than a clanging gong or clashing cymbal (1 Corinthians 13:1).

104. Love, according to the New Testament witness, is ever-widening, ever-deepening. When the early Christians were confronted with moral questions, they of course had recourse to the Hebrew Scriptures. But their primary reference was to Christ; their primary resource was the heart. They were not naive; they knew the heart can be devious. It can mislead, tempt, and endanger us. But while that is true, these problems of the heart were not the primary worry of Jesus. Jesus was much more worried about external religion

and its appeals to abstract authority, even to so-called biblical authority, than he was about the authority of the heart that seeks God. The more reliable test for truth in the early Christian community was to watch a person's life. Does her life bear fruit worthy of the gospel? Does his life show the life of Christ within him? When most of the early Jewish Christians first came to faith, they couldn't imagine God's love extending to the Greeks and Romans. But when they began meeting Greeks and Romans and saw evidence of the Holy Spirit's presence in their lives, they were forced to change their minds. Thus the evangelistic mission to the Gentiles was born (Acts 11:1–18).

105. I suppose I should have known all this. I'd gone to seminary. I have a masters and a doctorate in theology. I've been a pastor for nearly two decades—reading, praying, and preaching these biblical texts daily. I'd confessed Jesus Christ as Lord and Savior. But up until now I hadn't really seen him as he is—not at Saint Paul saw him, as the One who is "to have first place in everything" (Col 1:18). I'd not really worshiped him as Saint John had worshiped him, falling at Christ's feet "as though dead;" Christ who placed his right hand on John and said, "'Do not be afraid; I am the first and the last, and the living one. I was dead, and see, I am alive forever and ever; and I have the keys of Death and of Hades,'" (Rev 1:17–18). But my eyes were opened when I, like Saul on the road to Damascus, was forced to look at Christ again and reevaluate what I believed and taught.

106. I now see that Jesus Christ is bigger and better than I'd ever dared imagine. God's revelation in Christ changes everything. And one of the biggest changes I've come to understand and live is what Jesus actually requires of those of

us who follow him in obedience. There's no long list of rules and regulations from Jesus for his followers. There's only one commandment, the Greatest Commandment, and it has two parts: love God, and love others. The New Testament shows the early church living out the trajectory of that command-ment—sometimes successfully, other times failing; often with words and actions of great beauty, other times with the shrill voice of the religious authorities that persecuted them. But the early Christians were learning not to merely judge people by outer appearances[1]—appearances, they knew all too well, could be deceiving. Instead, following Jesus, they learned to discern faithfulness by the character of their lives; they tested the quality of the tree by its fruit (Luke 6:44). In our day, the gay people I know love well. Many of them are passionate about God; they are compassionate toward those in need. In short, they bear fruit. Not all of them of course. But neither do all Baptists or all Presbyterians, for that mat-ter. We've got some real stinkers inside the church, and no one's pushing them out the door because their fruit is rotten. Straight people don't have a monopoly on fruitfulness. And they don't get a pass in Jesus' eyes just because they're straight. So should gay Christians be excluded simply because they're gay? Should they be denied the spiritual benefits afforded to straight Christians?

107. If we follow the trajectory of Jesus's Greatest Com-mandment, the center of New Testament faith, I believe we're on shaky ground if we block gays and lesbians from full inclusion in the church. They can love God and love their

1. As Saint Paul says in 2 Corinthians 5:16–17: "From now on, therefore, we regard no one from a human point of view; even though we once knew Christ from a human point of view, we know him no longer in that way. So if anyone is in Christ, there is a new creation: everything old has passed away; see, everything has become new!"

neighbors just like the best straight people around. They can live the compassion of Jesus as well as anyone else can. Someone will say, "Well, the Bible says . . ." *Does* it? After the survey I've done, that's no more certain than saying the Bible teaches that the earth is the center of the solar system. Jesus Christ is our Bible now, not Leviticus. And Christ says, "Love one another as I have loved you" (John 15:12). That's why we cannot say to gay and lesbian persons, "God loves you, but . . ." There is no "but" to God's kind of loving. Christian love can no longer exclude gays and lesbians from baptism and holy communion, marriage and ordination. Excluding them makes our words sound hopelessly hollow, like a "clanging gong" (1 Cor 13:1). In my mouth, words of exclusion taste like sour fruit plucked from a pretty but rotten tree.

108. But there's one final reason I see full inclusion as a mandate of the gospel. The Greatest Commandment urges me to live a life of love and welcome all who seek to abide in Christ's love. But it's the New Testament's vision of the new creation that grounds this inclusion in solid, evangelical theology.

109. Saint Paul is the most articulate preacher of this vision, though the new creation is present among the other writers who speak of it differently. Both John and Peter, for example, use the phrase "the new birth" (John 3:3; 1 Pet 1:3). Mark simply calls it "the beginning of the good news" (Mark 1:1). The "new creation" is the core of the gospel Paul proclaimed, the reason for the possibility—or better, the *guarantee*—of the reconciliation, reunion, and wholeness of creation when it is summed up in Christ (2 Cor 5:16–21; Eph 1:10). In Christ, all things are being gathered up, Paul says—pulled together, cleansed, purified, and justified. In Christ, all creation is

irrepressibly being drawn into the direction of this fullness (Rom 8:18–25; Eph 1:9–10; Phil 2:9–11; Col 1:15–20).

110. In Jesus Christ, a new beginning has come—and it's every bit as dramatic and transformative as the first creation (Genesis 1). "In Christ, there is a new creation: everything old has passed away; see, everything has become new!" (2 Cor 5:17). In Christ, God is reconciling all things (Col 1:20), gathering up all that was once scattered (Eph 1:10), breaking down every wall that separates us from one another and from God (Eph 2:14), and is "abolishing the law with its commandments and ordinances" (Eph 2:15). All this is "built upon the foundation of the apostles and prophets, with Christ Jesus himself as the keystone" (Eph 2:20). And now, in Christ, "the whole structure is joined together and grows into a holy temple in the Lord; in whom you also are built together spiritually into a dwelling place for God" (Eph 2:21).

111. With the dawning of the *event* of Jesus Christ, "the fullness of time" has come (Gal 4:4). And in this new era, "there is no longer Jew or Greek, there is no longer slave or free, there is no longer male or female; for all of you are one in Christ Jesus. And if you belong to Christ, then you are Abraham's offspring, heirs according to the promise" (Gal 3:28–29). Beginning with Abraham and Sarah, the gift of inclusion into God's family has been spreading, the invitation to belong to the family of God extending. Even at the beginning there were hints and whispers of this trajectory (Gen 12:1–3; 13:14–16). And there were many others along the way (especially in Isaiah: 42:1–9; 49:1–6; 54:1–3; 56:3–8). These hints and whispers pointed to that one great eruption of the fullness of God's new governance in Jesus Christ. Now,

through the church, that eruption continues to widen and spread; the trajectory of God's reconciliation of all things is no longer a mere hint or whisper, but a mighty shout and force (Eph 1:11–22). All things are included. All things are coming together. This means that any tendency toward exclusion is a movement backward and is, therefore, antithetical to the gospel of Jesus Christ. In fact, any such movement is what the New Testament writers might call "anti-Christ" because such a movement moves against the evermore inclusive trajectory of the new creation.

112. This central theme of the New Testament is critically important because most discussions about homosexuality and Christian faith nearly always look backward, to the structures of creation. "God made Adam and Eve," many well-intentioned Christians say, "not Adam and Steve." But for a Christian, this is a terribly naive argument. Jesus and the apostles didn't look backward: they followed the trajectory of that past, with eyes firmly fixed on the future—the End, with a capital *E*. And that End is the fullness of all things reconciled in Christ.

113. In the Bible there are two contrasting visions of the End. First, there's the vision of a cataclysmic judgment and the salvation of a select few, and second, there's the vision of universal harmony and the salvation of a lot more. While not ignorant or dismissive of the first view, the Reformed tradition (along with most of orthodox Christianity) has favored the second, the union of all things in Christ. The first view, cataclysmic judgment, has been the playground of too many nuts and kooks who have led large numbers of people astray declaring that the End has come (we've seen a number of these come and go in the last few years). We must not follow

those who say "'Look! Here is the Messiah!' or 'Look! There he is!'" (Mark 13:21). We are to remain alert and watchful, though not fearful. For Christ will come "with great power and glory. Then he will send out the angels, and gather his elect from the four winds, from the ends of the earth to the ends of heaven" (Mark 13:26–27). Not one single person who has loved Christ and been loved by Christ will be left out. "No one who believes in him will be put to shame. For there is no distinction between Jew and Greek; the same Lord is Lord of all and is generous to all who call on him. For, 'Everyone who calls on the name of the Lord shall be saved'" (Rom 10:11–13).

114. We can't dismiss this vision of cataclysmic judgment and exclusion just because it's been misinterpreted so badly throughout history—though these abuses ought to make us wary to push too hard in its direction. But there are problems with the second view as well. The vision of universal harmony can make us too optimistic, too naive about sin and evil in the world. We must not forget that there are still plenty of reasons to temper our optimism about the future. Humanity is plenty able to wound itself, resist God's reign on earth, and wreak havoc on our planet.

115. Nevertheless, while there are things in this world that seem to pull us backward, threaten our lives, and give us reason for despair, we can also see a maturing, growing, and evolving of humanity. There are, of course, those who still favor the cataclysmic view of the End, and who will see even the positive signs of our emerging humanity as smoke screens for Satan's blinding of everyone except God's chosen ones who will be raptured from the earth before the Great Tribulation. But didn't Jesus tell us that the seed of God's

reign is relentlessly growing in the world, even among so many weeds, and that it would grow to become the greatest of all growing things, with many branches for birds of all kinds to make a home (Mark 4:30–32)? The tree is growing; God's house is expanding. It is irrepressible. No force can stand against it (John 1:5).

116. Despite the setbacks and threats, there is evidence all around us of this expanding, this new creation at work. Most people now have positive experiences with people very different from themselves. This wasn't true even a hundred years ago. Jews and Christians, Hindus and Muslims and atheists live side by side with each other. Immigrants from Europe and the Middle East, Asia and Africa and Central America know each other at work and school. Many of us see more similarities than differences, more reasons to cooperate than to argue or fight. More and more people realize that the problems that plague our planet require more cooperation, not less—that we need each other not just to thrive, but to survive.

117. My eyesight, now more fully formed by the gospel than ever before, sees more and more evidence of our planet itself being pulled into God's future. I'm not naive to the counterforces of sin, death, and evil that can seem rampant. My head is not in the sand. The forces of good and beauty and holiness are being challenged by a darkness that's rising to the challenge. But trained by the gospel, that gloom is not all I see. Instead, I see great movements of generosity and compassion among us; there are great ideas and technologies that link more people together than ever before; there's a more universal sense of what is just and good, and a commitment to work together to share in the future of this planet; and

there's a greater sense of the inherent dignity of each human person. A few generations ago, your ancestors could have owned slaves and thought nothing of it. A single generation ago, if you were black you'd have had to step off the sidewalk to make way for a white man, or give up your seat on a bus. But today, a black man holds the most powerful political office in the world, and a young Pakistani girl, shot by the Taliban while sitting on a school bus, has stirred international outrage and passionate support for women's rights in places where religion and culture still elevate men as superior to women. And finally, increasing numbers of people today see no reason to disallow two adults who love each other, regardless of their gender, from giving themselves to that partnership we call marriage. Some, it is true, see these as signs of apostasy, and the rise of the antichrist. But the New Testament theology of the new creation in Christ will not allow such an interpretation. Rather, all these are signs of the presence and power of Jesus Christ in the world, drawing it to its fullness in God.

118. The Greatest Commandment is the centerpiece of Jesus' teaching, and the theological vision of the new creation is the keystone of the New Testament. Love is what we do. And love is where we're headed. So, I'm an evangelist of these things. And what I've learned among my congregation, in my family, and through a quarter century of pastoral experience leads me to affirm the full equality and inclusion of gay and lesbian persons in the life of the church. They are not second-tier human beings, but are signs of what God is up to—to bring all things together in Christ. All are included at God's table of abundance, included in this ever-expanding circle of friends who live the Greatest Commandment and are signs of the new creation in Christ.

119. That said, there are still a lot of people who disagree with me—even some in my own congregation. Nevertheless, I am as convinced of this as Copernicus must have been when he looked up from his scientific studies and realized that the sun was, in fact, the center of the solar system—regardless of what the church taught. I am as committed to this as Wilberforce must have been when he looked into the eyes of African slaves and decided that he could no longer allow one human being to enslave another—no matter what the church taught. To me, holding the traditional view regarding homosexuality is like arguing that the sun revolves around the earth or that the enslavement of one human being by another is sanctioned by God. I fully realize that it took many long years until outdated views about the solar system and slavery died out. And so, I do not anticipate the changes I envision to come quickly, though I pray they do. Perhaps what I've written here will help speed these changes along and bring us all into the fullness of the gospel of Jesus Christ.

"Maranatha! Amen. Come, Lord Jesus!
The grace of the Lord Jesus be with all the saints. Amen."

REVELATION 22:20–21

6

Now What?

120. First, as a pastor, I am the spiritual shepherd to people who hold varying positions and perspectives on many things—social, political, and religious. I am responsible to God and to those under my care to guide all of them, to the best of my ability, into the fullness of Jesus Christ. When my conscience allows me to, I avoid preaching a political position aligned with a particular party or agenda. And whenever possible I seek to avoid polarizing the church over issues. People I care for deeply hold very different positions from me on a variety of things. I hold to the principle that difference of opinion is not a danger to life in community, but a guarantee of its health. This is true not only in the church, but in the public life of a democratic society. So, I do not intend to make my position *the* sole position of any congregation I serve. And I don't think what I argue for here should be the sole position of any church. There must be, in every congregation, room for dissent and debate. We are better for it, and faithfulness to the gospel demands it. I simply wish to be able to hold my position firmly while allowing others to

hold theirs. I want to be understood and valued even if others disagree with me. I have always valued opposing views, learned from them, and welcomed them to the table. I would like the same grace afforded to me. I would like dialogue and debate, mixed with respect and humor. The church must be a community that works, through our various perspectives on Jesus Christ, to discern the will of God in our time and place. The point is, I won't communicate that my position is the official position of the church, though I will hold it with conviction and live it out for the sake of God's justice.

121. Second, regarding same-gender marriage: I will treat the marriages of all couples, whether gay or straight, equally. I will not marry any couple simply because they ask me to marry them. Marriage is sacred. That is, it is a sign of the of the way of union—through learning to love another, we learn to love God; and through learning to love God, we learn to love one another. We Protestants don't consider marriage a sacrament, but it seems to me we ought to move more fully in that direction if we are to rediscover the wonder and power of marriage in an age of such confusion and brokenness. The union of our human lives in marriage is a sign of that union with the divine we are all made for, the intimacy we all seek. So, I aim to affirm, promote, and protect the sanctity of marriage. This means that straight or gay, I will discern the readiness of every couple for the great gift marriage is for our families, our communities, and our individual souls. Is there evidence that this couple is on the path of Christian discipleship? Are they aware of the joyous and challenging commitments they're planning to make? Do they have the spiritual resources to make marriage work? Will their marriage be a sign—regardless of the struggles they will face, the

weaknesses and failures—of the reconciliation and wholeness of God that is now among us in Jesus Christ?

122. Third, we need to have more robust conversations not
just about gay marriage, but about marriage in general. What
is marriage, *really*? What is marriage in the Bible, in Christian faith, in contemporary society? Marriage today certainly doesn't look like marriage did in the time of Noah or
Abraham (thank God), David, Jesus, the Puritans, or Queen
Victoria. It doesn't look the same today in India as it does
in Indiana. Marriage in Marrakesh looks a lot different than
it does in Minnesota. We need to ask, "How do the Greatest Commandment and the new creation shape marriage
today and help us strengthen the families of the twenty-first
century?" Is there a sacramentalism we Protestants ought
to discover in order to find the resources necessary to live
robust and vibrant lives *because* we are married to a partner
who can help us experience the presence of God? And, of
course, conversations about marriage must include sexuality as well. Sex isn't going away, and, sadly, most of us aren't
very good at it, despite our fascination with it. Part of the
problem is that the church by and large has avoided talking
about sex, and people are suffering. So, what do we believe
about sex as Christians? How can we foster sexual practices
that are healthy, robust, and truly *re*-creational? What is sex
for? Who is it for? And as we learn more about sexuality, how
can we bring the light of the gospel to our sexuality? We're
currently locked in debate over homosexuality, but people of
all kinds ache in loneliness and repressed desires that create
all kinds of confusion, wounding, and brokenness.

123. Fourth, we need to develop and embrace a healthier theology of the Holy Trinity. As Christians, we are Trinitarian

believers. But for most Christians, the Trinity is an odd doc-trine—confusing, sometimes embarrassing, and better left to professionals. But the Trinity is immensely practical. God-as-Trinity, three persons *yet* one being, offers us a clue to what it means to live as human beings in community. God-as-Trinity, fully differentiated *yet* united, also extends the promise that healthy and flourishing relationships are, in fact, possible. So, "if God can get along," I often tell our congregation, "then we can too!" The Trinity is not merely a theological doctrine, but a way to live. The nature of God as community is a gift to the nature of human community. The nature of God can influence not only the way we live in Christian congregations and families, but also how we relate to others in society and to the planet itself. This also means that the Trinity has direct bearing on our conversations about marriage, homosexuality, and the gospel. Traditional-ists often argue that marriage *must* be between a man and a woman because "God created humankind in his image, in the image of God he created them; male and female he cre-ated them" (Gen 1:27). Two married men or two married women, they argue, cannot experience the complementarity God intends. But, to me, this seems to miss an important Christian truth. It fails to embrace the implications the of na-ture of God as Trinity. God-as-Trinity reveals that no one ex-ists in isolation, not even God. What's more, it declares that complementarity is not merely found in duality—between *two* persons. Rather, the Trinity shows us that community is always *more* than two. Father, Son, *and* Holy Spirit. To say that a gay couple can't be complete seems to me to miss the relational significance of the Trinity. If the Trinity is the true image of God, then the image of God is not primarily about gender—that is, "male and female." It's about plurality and unity and relationship. It's about the fact that at the deepest parts of our being we yearn for communion. And so, the image of God is always two *plus*. God in the mix. God, the sacred Third. And if God is the Third in a marriage of two, why, then, can't a gay or lesbian couple live in health and holiness with God among them, the triune One who always brings to our relationships the fullness of communion we were made to enjoy?

124. Fifth, the church hasn't had serious conversations about ordination to church office—pastor, elder, deacon—for centuries. We've not explored what ordination means today in light of a more highly educated population, people who have a remarkable amount of access to information and technology, and the experience of a broadening democracy. What does ordination mean in light of the emergence of new forms of authority, credentialing, leadership development/training, and community formation? What is leadership within society and the church? How are leaders formed? Where do they derive their authority? What is the role of holiness, virtue, and wisdom, and how are they formed? We need to ask, "What is 'the church' itself in this new setting?" And, then: "What is leadership?" "What is ordination?" "Who shall we ordain and for what?" These are the kinds of conversations we must have if the church is not only to survive the twenty-first century, but is to thrive in the ever-expanding fullness of Jesus Christ.

A Guide for Reflection
and Conversation

Having simple conversations with others is a remarkable way to not only discover how others view things, but to better understand and articulate our own views. Unfortunately, real conversations are exceedingly rare today. What could be conversations often turn into shouting matches, and pseudoconversations online mislead people into thinking they're actually talking with others. But these aren't real conversations; they leave us dissatisfied, sometimes downright wounded. And they're certainly not ways for Christians to explore truth. So I hope you'll relearn a practice so basic to being human—essential to being Christian.

Here are a few tips for hosting the kinds of conversations that can help us all thrive as Christians. When we meet for conversation:

- We affirm that we are all made in the image of God, as equals and allies, not competitors

- We agree that curiosity about each other is more fruitful than indifference or close-mindedness

- We remember that Jesus taught by engaging in real, honest conversation with others

- We acknowledge that Jesus promises that where we gather in community, he is present in the Spirit

- We realize that listening can be difficult and so we need each others' help
- We want to learn to slow down, think, reflect, feel
- We agree to use "I" statements, owning our own ideas, and giving others freedom to express theirs
- We expect conversation to be messy and unpredictable as well as rewarding and enriching

A GUIDE TO CHAPTER 1: A TESTIMONY AND JUSTIFICATION

1. In paragraphs 1–3, the author tells the tale of two weddings, the first, a very traditional wedding in a church between two young men, and the second, a more modern wedding outside the church between a young man and woman. The first raised questions for a number of those invited; some of them declined to attend, "on principle." The second wedding raised no questions at all. Those who declined to attend declined because they had other commitments, not reservations about the marriage itself. The truth is, "an increasing number of Americans" are asking new questions about gay marriage (paragraph 4). What kinds of questions do the stories of these two weddings raise for you?

2. In 2010, the author's congregation engaged in a long congregational study called "The Bible and Homosexuality." This is a moderately conservative congregation in

one of the most conservative regions in California. It wanted to "lay out the issues and explore them fully, but not to promote one view over the other" (paragraph 10). If your congregation or community were to plan a way to engage the topic of God, the Bible, and homosexuality, how would they go about it? What do you think should be included? Is there anything you'd exclude from the conversation?

3. Evangelists often get a bad rap in our society. In paragraph 17, the author says, "Evangelists don't just preach a heavenly message of hope in the hereafter. . . . [They] bring change, and there have always been opponents who don't like the fact that they 'who have turned the world upside down have come here too' (Acts 17:6)." What, then, is a true evangelist? Can you name an evangelist from some period in history who you think represented the gospel well? What did he or she do? How was her or his message received? What challenges did the evangelist face? What was the long-term fruit of the evangelist's life and message?

4. In paragraph 22, the author says that he wants to cultivate "a community where anyone drawn to Christ receives

an unmistakable, unqualified invitation to come and eat at the table of the Lord among an ever-growing circle of friends." How does this sound to you? How consistent is it with your understanding of the gospel? Are there limits you'd to place around this table? Are there any requirements for behavior or belief you'd put in place before allowing others to sit down at the feast? What are they and why are they important to you?

5. What in this section troubles you? Why?

6. What do you find interesting and intriguing?

A GUIDE TO CHAPTER 2: THE BIBLE SAYS IT, DOES THAT SETTLE IT?

1. In paragraph 25, the author says "People have done crazy things by reading the Bible without wisdom." In this section, he explores the way his congregation wanted to

approach the Bible with an awareness of the opinions, prejudices, and agendas that we bring to our Bible reading. Can you talk about an example of the way the Bible has been used to support a particular personal or political agenda? If you could identify the interpretive "lens" you've inherited what would it be—that is, what are one or two assumptions you bring to your Bible reading?

2. It's easy, of course, to say, "The Bible says it," but an honest look at parts of the Old Testament, for example, make it clear that interpreting these ancients texts is anything but easy. The author says that "most of us walk among these laws the way we walk through a line at a cafeteria—we pick and choose what we like or that's useful to us, and ignore the rest" (paragraph 34). Later he says that "this review of the key texts . . . loosened many of us from the answers we once thought were so assured by the Bible" (paragraph 37). How do these two statements make you feel? How do you think we can hold the Bible's authority in tension with the reality that interpreting it can be just plain tough and so often susceptible to our biases?

3. In paragraphs 35 and 36, the author argues that in selections from key New Testament texts prohibiting homosexuality, Saint Paul was not referring to the kind of "monogamous, faithful relationships our gay friends and family members enjoy or would like to enjoy." In what ways might this truth invite you to ask deeper questions than you've asked before? Can you talk about a time in your work history or personal experience when new information changed the way you did your job or lived your life?

4. Jesus handled Scripture differently than the scribes and Pharisees around him did. "The Gospels show Jesus to be remarkably willing to dismiss scriptural laws when they were causing injury to others." "What is clear from the New Testament is that Christians, like Jesus, must practice an artful interpretive dance as we read the law in the light of the gospel" (paragraph 38). This can seem arbitrary and can make people who are serious about the Bible uncomfortable. Read Mark 3:1–6 and talk about how the religious people around Jesus must have felt, what they might have thought, and how you might have reacted to Jesus had you been among them.

5. What in this section troubles you? Why?

6. What do you find interesting and intriguing?

A GUIDE TO CHAPTER 3: WHY WE NEED HISTORY AND REASON

1. In paragraph 47, the author summarizes a practice for interpreting Scripture that's particularly Protestant, but is shared, in principle, among Catholic and Orthodox Christians. Faithful Christian interpretation, he says, is "an artful dance between our sacred texts, Jesus as revealed in those texts, history, the cultural context we find ourselves in, our own experience, and the presence and guidance of the Holy Spirit." His congregation explored historical case studies alongside relevant texts from Scripture in their study of the Bible and homosexuality: the christological controversies (fourth and fifth centuries), cosmology (sixteenth and seventeenth centuries), the slave trade (eighteenth and nineteenth centuries), and the role and authority of women in the church (nineteenth and twentieth centuries). Talk about the way scientific discovery, for example, challenged the

views Martin Luther held about the relationship of the sun and earth (paragraph 55), and why you think it may have taken the church so long to admit the need to change its views.

2. In another case, the problem of Christian support of slavery, the author says that "using biblical texts alone in order to argue against slavery was a daunting task" (paragraph 58). Very few people today, especially Christians, support the practice of enslaving other human beings. If you denounce slavery, how do you explain your conviction when so much of the Bible supports the practice?

3. There are religious movements today that worry about the moral relativism of our day, the loss of faith in organized religion. Those who are part of them want greater certainty and look to the Bible to give them that. But the author says that there's a necessary freedom to faithful Christian interpretation. "It's this liberated, live-by-the-Spirit-not-the-law kind of religion (Gal 5:16) that got Saint Paul into such trouble with those who wanted more certainty, clearer rules" (paragraph 62). What do you feel you need today—on a scale of 1 to 10, do you

need clearer answers or more freedom to explore Christian faith in the modern world (1 is absolute certainty and 10 is total freedom)?

4. The author is concerned that some Christians are "too willing to see the absence of God rather than the presence of God" in the world around us (paragraph 64). He says that Scripture and history show us that "the Holy Spirit was often out in front of God's people, 'doing a new thing' (Isa 43:16), revealing the will of God outside the church before the church itself was able to see the 'new thing' God intended to do (Acts 10)" (paragraph 65). Can you talk about what you think Christianity might be like today if our ancestors had resisted the pressure to change, a pressure that was coming at them from outside the church? What are one or two guidelines you'd suggest Christians use to discern when it is necessary to resist the voices of change that come from outside the church?

5. What in this section troubles you? Why?

6. What do you find interesting and intriguing?

A GUIDE TO CHAPTER 4: THE PASTORAL AND
MISSIONAL SITUATION

1. "Personal encounter is the opener of eyes," writes the author in paragraph 70. He points to William Wilberforce as an example. "'At age twenty-six and at the height of his political career, something profound and dramatic happened to him. . . . [H]e saw God's reality—what Jesus called the Kingdom of Heaven. . . . He saw the idea that all men and women are created by God, in his image, and are therefore sacred'" (paragraph 70). Can you talk about a time when a personal encounter with someone different from you opened your eyes to see things in ways that are, in retrospect, more true to God's ways than what you saw or believed before that experience?

2. In paragraph 76, the author says that "a truly *evangelical* theology . . . doesn't dabble in abstractions, it doesn't pretend to be objective." The Bible itself is evidence of the way relationships change our theology (see examples in paragraph 77). Talk about the way personal

relationships affect your beliefs (paragraph 80). If you or someone you love has served in the military, are you more apt to support military force as a means to peace? If you're a hunter, does your your experience as a hunter affect your opinion on gun control? If you know a hard-working Mexican family, does that relationship affect your opinion on immigration? Why or why not?

3. "If you get to know gay people and learn of the trouble they have trying to find their bearings in their families, schools, and work settings, you'll come face-to-face with the massive challenges before them" (paragraph 78). "You never know whether or not anyone you're living with may be living with a secret they've never found the courage to tell you about" (paragraph 79). What is your personal experience with a person who happens to be gay? What is your personal experience with a family who has a gay family member? Talk about what you know of that person or family's story, and what the reality of homosexuality has meant for their lives.

4. Mission and evangelism have been powerful forces of change historically. The author gives some examples in paragraph 86. Current statistics reveal that nearly 60

percent of the young people raised in the church will walk way from it as adults (paragraphs 84 and 85). And more than 80 percent of them "believe that Christians show excessive contempt and unloving attitudes towards gays and lesbians." Some Christians believe that today's youth are misguided and that the church must not capitulate its beliefs to this moral decay; Christians must hold more firmly to their traditional beliefs. Others believe "the church is too preoccupied with self-preservation" and must follow Jesus more daringly into the world and be less afraid of it (paragraph 88). What do you think? Do you tend to lean more inward, looking toward the church itself and holding firm to what we've always believed? Or do you tend to lean outward, believing the Holy Spirit speaks to the church from the outside? What do you recommend the church do to reach today's disinterested youth with the gospel?

5. What in this section troubles you? Why?

6. What do you find interesting and intriguing?

A GUIDE TO CHAPTER 5: THE TRAJECTORY OF THE GREATEST COMMANDMENT AND THE NEW CREATION

1. In the first part of this chapter, the author is exploring the relationship between the Old Testament and the New, the law and the gospel. As he and his congregation studied these things, "we realized we needed to see that what the biblical writers knew of God grew and changed over the course of the Bible's history. Malachi has a more expanded vision than Moses. And what Isaiah glimpsed becomes a full reality to John the evangelist" (paragraph 93). In paragraph 95, he writes, "We can't minimize the effects of the dramatic change that has come in and through Jesus Christ." Reflect on your own relationship with the Old Testament—the Hebrew Scriptures. It's not too difficult as a Christian to make sense of the messianic promises in Isaiah and Malachi, but how do you make sense of God sending Joshua and his warriors to slaughter the inhabitants of Jericho (Josh 6)? In what ways do you see the knowledge of God evolving over the course of biblical history?

2. In a provocative passage, the author writes, "An honest reading of the New Testament showed me that the early Christians often seemed to play footloose and fancy free with the Hebrew Scriptures. They made audacious claims, taking things out of context, advocating what faithful Jews considered lunacy at best and heresy

at worst. But the disciples of Jesus came by it honestly; Jesus did it too. That's one of the things that got him killed" (paragraph 98). What is your response to what the author says in this section? What concerns might it raise? On the other hand, in what ways might his words help you make better sense of the relationship between the Old and the New?

3. "I now see," writes the author in paragraph 106, "that Jesus Christ is bigger and better than I'd ever dared imagine. God's revelation in Christ changes everything. And one of the biggest changes I've come to understand and live is what Jesus actually requires of those of us who follow him in obedience. There's no long list of rules and regulations from Jesus for his followers. There's only one command, the Greatest Commandment, and it has two parts: love God, and love others." In light of this, how do you respond to the problem he sees? "We've got some real stinkers inside the church," he writes, "and no one's pushing them out the door because their fruit is rotten. Straight people don't have a monopoly on fruitfulness. And they don't get a pass in Jesus' eyes just because they're straight. So should gay Christians be excluded simply because they're gay? Should they be denied the spiritual benefits afforded to straight Christians?" (paragraph 106). If the law of love is what we are to live, and if fruit bearing is the test of our obedience, do you think a person's sexual orientation is the criteria for including

or excluding someone from the Christian community and from full participation in it?

4. The author closes the chapter with a reflection the New Testament's keystone vision of the "new creation." "'In Christ, there is a new creation: everything old has passed away; see, everything has become new!' (2 Cor 5:17). In Christ, God is reconciling all things (Col 1:20), gathering up all that was once scattered (Eph 1:10), breaking down every wall that separates us from one another and from God (Eph 2:14), and is 'abolishing the law with its commandments and ordinances' (Eph 2:15)" (paragraph 110). To the author, this means that God's table of abundance is open for all people and that the church must become a sign of this "ever-expanding circle of friends who live the Greatest Commandment and are signs of the new creation in Christ" (paragraph 118). Reflect on whether or not you are moved by this vision to become more inclusive in your faith (in *any* way) as a sign of the new creation in Christ. If you are, what steps might you take next? If you're not, what are your key objections?

5. What in this section troubles you? Why?

6. What do you find interesting and intriguing?

A GUIDE TO CHAPTER 6: NOW WHAT?

1. The author believes it's not only possible for people within a congregation and in the broader church to hold different views, he argues that it's beneficial. "There must be, in every congregation, room for dissent and debate. We are better for it, and faithfulness to the gospel demands it" (paragraph 120). From your experience, talk about how and why difference of opinion is a good thing, something the gospel may even require. At the same time, do you think there are there limits to the breadth of dissent—that is, how wide can our differences be and still be considered part of the Christian faith? Where would you draw those lines?

2. In paragraphs 121 and 122, the author explores our need to have a more robust conversation about Christian marriage and sexuality. Nearly 50 percent of marriages

end in divorce. And the church rarely talks honestly about sex despite the fact that sex is on almost everyone's minds. In your experience, what has the church done to promote healthy marriages and teach a view of sexuality that is neither prudish nor promiscuous, but is vibrant and nourished from inside a safe, secure marital relationship?

3. About marriage in particular, the author says that "We need to ask, 'How do the Greatest Commandment and the new creation shape marriage today and help us strengthen the families of the twenty-first century?'" He urges us to see marriage more as a sacrament than a contract or social institution (paragraph 122). He also offers the kinds of questions he will ask of every couple, straight and gay, who seek Christian marriage. Explore the way this kind of commitment to the sacredness of marriage might make a difference in the Christian practice of marriage today.

4. "Traditionalists often argue that marriage must be between a man and a woman because 'God created humankind in his image, in the image of God he created them; male and female he created them' (Gen 1:27).

Two married men or two married women, they argue, cannot experience the complementarity God intends" (paragraph 123). The author then explores the doctrine of the Trinity and invites us to consider that the image of God may be "not primarily about gender—that is, 'male and female.'" Instead, it may be more "about plurality and unity and relationship." If this is true, how might the nature of God as Trinity change the way you think about marriage, and in particular, does it open you to the possibility of same-gender marriage?

5. Questions about homosexuality and Christian faith do not just impact marriage. They also influence what we believe about ordination to the offices of the church. In paragraph 124, the author says that the church hasn't had serious conversations about ordination in quite a long time. "We've not explored what ordination means today in light of a more highly educated population, people who have a remarkable access to information and technology, and the experience of a broadening democracy. What does ordination mean in light of the emergence of new forms of authority, credentialing, leadership development/training, and community formation?" It used to be that pastors were the most educated persons in a town or village. If education is no longer *the* distinguishing characteristic of a pastor, what is? And what are elders and deacons for, *really*? Most elders in Presbyterian churches are more like members of a board of directors or unpaid staff than the kind of

seasoned, wise saints envisioned in earlier times. What questions might you ask that could help the church explore ordination more fully today? What reasons might you give for excluding gays and lesbians from ordination? What reasons might you give for including them?

5. What in this section troubles you? Why?

6. What do you find interesting and intriguing?

Bibliography

The Barmen Declaration. *The Constitution of the Presbyterian Church (U.S.A.), Part 1, Book of Confessions.* Louisville: Office of the General Assembly Presbyterian Church (USA), 2004.

Barna Group. "A New Generation Expresses its Skepticism and Frustration with Christianity." https://www.barna.org/barna-update/teens-nextgen/94-a-new-generation-expresses-its-skepticism-and-frustration-with-christianity#.UvEz_HmuORQ.

———. "How Can We Reverse the Trend?" https://www.barna.org/labs#.U8Vo4lauNME.

———. "Six Reasons Young Christians Leave Church." https://www.barna.org/teens-next-gen-articles/528-six-reasons-young-christians-leave-church.

The Gilder Lehrman Institute of American History. "Lincoln Speech on Slavery and the American Dream, 1858." http://www.gilderlehrman.org/history-by-era/lincoln/resources/lincoln-speech-slavery-and-american-dream-1858.

Kinnaman, David. *unChristian: What a New Generation Really Thinks about Christianity . . . and Why It Matters.* Grand Rapids: Baker, 2012.

Kobe, Donald. "Copernicus and Martin Luther: An Encounter Between Science and Religion." *American Journal of Physics* 66 (3) 1998.

NPR. "'Amazing Grace' and the End of the Slave Trade." An excerpt from Eric Metaxas's *Amazing Grace: William Wilberforce and the Heroic Campaign to End Slavery.* San Francisco: Harper, 2007. http://www.npr.org/templates/story/story.php?storyId=7551106.

Pope Francis. "Apostolic Exhortation: Evangelii Gaudium of the Holy Father Francis to the Bishops, Clergy, Consecrated Persons and the Lay Faithful on the Proclamation of the Gospel in Today's World." http://w2.vatican.va/content/francesco/en/apost_exhortations/documents/papa-francesco_esortazione-ap_20131124_evangelii-gaudium.html#III.%E2%80%82The_new_evangelization_for_the_transmission_of_the_faith.

Rogers, Jack. *Presbyterian Creeds: A Guide to the Book of Confessions.* Louisville: Westminster John Knox, 1985.